MW01043454

A Maine Woman's Travel Letters:
MRS. HERMANN KOTZSCHMAR'S 1897 GRAND TOUR

JANICE PARKINSON-TUCKER

Longfellow Square.
Greetings from Portland, Maine.

Island Excursion Steamer "Pilgrim".
Greetings from Portland, Maine.

ISBN 0-9763041-0-4 Copyright ©2004 Casco House Publishing. All rights reserved.
Design by Univoice Graphics, Portland
Published by Casco House Publishing, 121 Pilgrim Road, South Portland, Maine 04106; jpt@maine.rr.com

Cover: Photograph of horse and carriage with (*from left to right*) Dorothea Kotzschmar, Smith College class of 1899, Emma Winchester, Class of 1900, and Georgina Montgomery, n.d. Photographer unknown. Courtesy of Smith College Archives; used with permission.

Back Cover: London Zoo postcard courtesy of Retrograve Archives; used with permission. Other images from the author's collection.

Acknowledgements

Anyone who goes through the process of creating a book for publication soon discovers that such a project is definitely a joint adventure shared with many people, each filling little slots until the whole picture emerges; it is like doing a huge jig-saw puzzle, sharing the fitting in of the individual pieces, until the entire scene is evident. It is really quite exciting.

Here are some of the people who have done their part along the way, helping to make this book a reality. It was William David Barry, Reference Librarian at the Maine Historical Society, who found the original short biographical article about Mrs. Kotzschmar which revealed the existence of her travel letters in a Portland newspaper. Then Tom Gaffney, Special Collections Librarian at the Portland Public Library, dug deep and found the newspapers in question, on microfilm. Tom Wilsbach, Art and Audiovisuals Librarian, also at the Portland Public Library, was very helpful about general information and postcard selection, and Richard Westland kindly advised me and secured many of the more interesting and rare postcards that are used in this book.

Postcards and illustrations were supplied by Mrs. Eric H. L. Sexton, Patty Savage, Rian Keating, Douglas Stover, John and Betty Mont, Smith College Archives, Maine Historical Society, Mystic Seaport Archives, First Parish in Portland Unitarian Universalist Church, The Library of Congress, and Retrograph Archive. I have used postcards from my private collection, and maps from my group of vintage *Baedeker* guides spanning the period 1894-1910.

I must thank the staff at Maine Historical Society, including Nicholas Noyes, Stephanie Philbrick, Don King, Matthew Barker, and Kathy Amoroso for their assistance, advice and encouragement. The Portland Public Library staff, especially from Periodicals, the Portland Room and the Reference Desk has continually been very patient and forthcoming as I pursued my research. I am also grateful to the Portland Rossini Club for allowing me to examine their earliest records, from 1869.

I have had valuable assistance from Dawn Berry, Ray Cornils, Nancy Ehlers, Barbara Fox, Anne Gilbert, Dorothy Hansen, Bill Marshall, Beth Marshall, Sylvia Nickels, Barbara Pruitt, Carol Robison, Eric Robison, Gaetano Santa Lucia, and Bonnie Studdiford.

Katie Murphy of Univoice Graphics has spent untold hours designing this book. She has been totally enthusiastic and creative about the work, and I am grateful to her.

The biggest ovation goes to my husband, James S. Tucker, who has listened to me talk, dream about and ponder over Mrs. Kotzschmar continually for more than a year now. He listened, gave advice when asked, and never doubted my work—he has believed in it from the beginning. His support has made this book a worthy goal and a real pleasure .

Thank you, everyone!

—Janice Parkinson-Tucker

This book

has been issued

as a

limited edition.

This is Number *113* of 250.

Jasmin Parkinson-Tucker

by the author

Contents

DEDICATION

THIS BOOK IS DEDICATED
TO THE SPIRIT OF
ADVENTURE
IN EVERY WOMAN.

FOREWORD

IN APRIL OF 1897 MRS. HERMANN KOTZSCHMAR OF PORTLAND, MAINE made her first, eagerly anticipated trip to Europe. She traveled with seven others from Maine, including her daughter Dorothea, who was between her second and third year of study at Smith College. During her five months away Mrs. Kotzschmar sent 23 letters back to Portland's *Daily Press* and to *The Kennebec Journal* in Augusta. It was customary in this period for travelers to keep a diary, either in the form of a personal journal or as letters to family. It was more unusual to send such letters back to the local newspaper.

I became interested in Mrs. Kotzschmar (1853-1937) while researching her husband Hermann Kotzschmar (1829-1908), a German immigrant who became a noted musician in Portland; in fact, the city's famed Kotzschmar Memorial Organ was dedicated to his memory in 1912.

Naturally, while reading about Hermann Kotzschmar, I also became interested in his family. It was in a large volume called *Representative Women of New England,* edited in 1904 by Julia Ward Howe, that I discovered a reference to travel letters that Mrs. Kotzschmar sent home to the local newspaper from her first trip out of the country.

The Portland Public Library's collections include the *Daily Press* on microfilm through October of 1897, so I was able to locate the

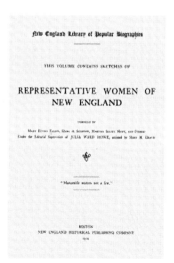

letters, copy, then transcribe and edit them. I found that Mrs. Kotzschmar sent back one lengthy letter a week, from mid-April until mid-September. The newspapers printed a disclaimer following the end of the first letter:

"The PRESS will publish from time to time letters from Mrs. Kotzschmar describing her tour through Europe. These letters will probably appear weekly, the one we publish above is a guarantee that they will be bright, interesting and well worth reading."

Twenty-two more letters, one written each week, were actually published. Mrs. Kotzschmar was home by the time the last article appeared on October 9, 1897, and was able to read the final entry in the newspaper herself.

THE LETTERS

Mrs. Hermann Kotzschmar's travel letters, in the best tradition of 19th century travel literature, are long, rich in detail, carefully crafted and full of literary and classical allusions. Each one made frequent references to characters and places from literature, music, history, art, mythology and religion, and often required an explanation for readers of today. Mrs. Kotzschmar married young and had no formal college or university experience, but she was obviously well read, comfortable with the classics and expected her readers to be the same.

She certainly did not seem to lack for material to construct her fascinating account. The travelers had abundant shifts of venue and many adventures; she probably had some hard decisions to make about which ones to write home. Mrs. Kotzschmar no doubt sent back her reports in long-hand, and could not have had much opportunity to proofread and revise them.

THE ITINERARY

The journey appears to have been well-thought-out, so that time and money were used to best advantage in visiting the places most important to the travelers. Included were visits to major sites of interest in each of the countries visited: England, Scotland, France, Switzerland, Italy, Germany, Belgium and Holland. The sites selected for visiting on this first trip abroad reveal Mrs. Kotzschmar's strong background and active interest in the cultural world. During the course of the trip the group visited several places associated with great writers, including Shakespeare's home in Avon, Sir Walter Scott's grave at Dryburgh Abbey, a visit to the grave of George Eliot in Highgate Cemetery, and the churchyard at Stoke Poges, where Gray wrote his famous *Elegy*.

The group also heard musical performances by world-class artists in London, Paris, Dresden and Bayreuth. The travelers visited museums and art galleries, attended the theatre and a variety of concerts, saw the homes of several famous literary figures and visited the birth houses of major composers. They also took time to visit areas of great natural beauty such as the Isle of Wight (off the southern coast of England), Exmoor in Devon (this trip being inspired, I think, by the lengthy novel *Lorna Doone* by R. D. Blackmore), and the Bay of Sorrento.

In Mrs. Kotzschmar's enthusiastic view the important parts of the trip were the dramatic and every-changing landscapes and the artistic and cultural satisfactions she found in her destinations. She appears healthy, hearty, good-natured and ready for any adventure that might present itself, describing, but not dwelling on the physical inconveniences such as   bad weather, long train trips and crossing the English Channel. Given the challenges of travel in 1897 with horse-drawn vehicles, steam trains and huge steamer trunks packed with bulky clothing, it seems amazing today in the age of air travel, suitcases on wheels and wash-and-wear clothing, that the party accomplished as much as is recorded in the five months that they were away from home. In 1897 women dressed in long skirts, multiple petticoats, large hats, gloves, and all the lady-like accessories that constituted haute couture—certainly not the most comfortable traveling and sightseeing attire in summer months.

Indeed, it is a daunting exercise to conjure up the inconveniences, delays and even dangers that the travelers might have faced in 1897. Long lines and security checks in today's airports seem temporary inconveniences compared to European train travel back then. Travelers endured narrow wooden seats without plush cushions, no shock absorbers, and the possibility that windows would not even open for ventilation in hot summer weather. Nor did the trains move along very quickly, due in part to uneven rail beds and impediments along the track. Mrs. Kotzschmar's cheerfulness and optimism probably endeared her to her companions more than once on the trip.

This trip must have been physically strenuous considering all the walking the Maine travelers did in places like Devon, the Isle of Wight, Pompeii, and even just around the cities they visited. I believe that the group members were in very fit condition and intended to stay that way—they did, for example, admit to spending June 21, the day before Queen Victoria's Jubilee Celebration, "dallying with dumb-bells, Indian clubs and sand-bags."

Physical fitness was an important consideration for the "modern" woman of the 1890s, and the women on this five month tour would have had to be in good shape to keep up with their plans. They apparently took few days off for catching their breath or restoring flagging energies.

THE GRAND TOUR

I am referring to this trip as *"Mrs. Kotzschmar's Grand Tour"* because she followed in the traditional path of the classic journey of the same name. The concept of the Grand Tour began in the 17th century when young Englishmen would spend two or more years traveling in Europe. The Grand Tour was designed to broaden horizons by providing travelers with immersion in foreign languages, art, architecture, geography, and music. Perhaps private study with foreign masters would be included, to enhance a person's goals of general artistic, cultural and personal enrichment and/or artistry. The trip usually focused on cities that were considered to be centers of culture such as Paris, Venice, Rome, Milan, Naples and Florence. As time went on the original concept of the Grand Tour was modified and reshaped. Women became interested in independent foreign travel, and there are now very good accounts of their ventures into what was once considered totally male territory.

For Americans especially, the Grand Tour was an invaluable education in the "Old World." Such a trip gave new world tourists a grasp of history that could never be duplicated by simply reading. In the same way that the English were fascinated by Paris and life on the Continent, Americans were very keen to visit London and perhaps continue on to the Continent. Mrs. Kotzschmar referred to London as "a world in itself" and that is where she started her adventure. After three months she went on to explore the mainland of Europe. London was her "port of entry" into the "Old World."

A taste of travel often creates a hunger for even more travel. Mrs. Kotzschmar did repeat her European journey, revisiting some areas and also branching out to other places to broaden her experiences and continuing education. She again went to Europe in 1900 and 1903. Ellis Island records reveal that Mrs. Kotzschmar and her daughter, by then Dorothea Sachsee (and husband Arthur), came into New York from Cherbourg on the S. S. Deutschland on September 3, 1909. Dorothea wrote in the Smith College reunion book "…we returned from a most delightful summer in Europe in 1909…"

MRS. HERMANN KOTZSCHMAR

A spouse or partner of a person in the public eye becomes a "silent partner," standing in the background and reflected light of the more prominent person. This was especially so in earlier times, before women began to speak out actively and openly for their own sakes. "Trained" by their grandfathers, fathers, brothers and older women in the family to be good companions rather than forthright personalities, women learned that their interests and desires had to take second place to those of their spouse, and found that their needs and wants often diminished in importance as male children matured. These "silent partners" did not stand on their own merits and accomplishments but were identified primarily by their connection to the more famous family members. Often they kept life organized and flowing, as is typified in the old saying "behind every great man there is a woman." In this tradition, our subject always referred to herself as "Mrs. Hermann Kotzschmar" rather than Mary Ann Torrey Kotzschmar.

The Kotzschmars were married on December 16, 1872, the bride's nineteenth birthday. The groom was 43. This age difference of 24 years, more than one full generation, though not out of character in that time period, would set up a certain deference to the elder partner. The natural respect that is paid to a person of stature must also have played a role. Not until her gravestone was carved in 1937 was this lady presented to the world as "Mary A. Kotzschmar." (There is but one exception to this, and it is in the records of Portland's Rossini Club, which will be discussed below.) She was very proud to be "Mrs. Hermann Kotzschmar."

On the other hand, it is clear in her travel letters that she was a woman ahead of her time, and she supported the causes of femininity; for example, in the last travel letter she writes:

> "We know there must be many women who long for Europe, as Moses did for Canaan, and fear to die without the sight; not always on account of slender purses but often from lack of courage in going alone and unprotected. To some extent we shared these fears at first, but they soon vanished. English is so universally spoken, and more than all traveling is made easy by means of the "International Pensions" distributed throughout the principal resorts of Europe, where for a reasonable sum comfortable accommodations can be secured for one night or longer."

I would be very interested in what else Mrs. Kotzschmar would say on the subject of women traveling, if we could engage her in a conversation of more length. In this brief paragraph she has covered the major areas of money, language differences and safe accommodations. She was a practical lady.

Mary Ann Torrey was born in Sacramento, California in 1853. Her parents, both Maine natives, lived in Deer Isle, a tiny fishing community on the Downeast coast. In 1849 her father, Midian, "got the gold fever and went 'round the Horn." In fact, he was one of the "original '49ers." His wife, Mary Ann, and two young sons Ebenezer P. and Charles H. went along on the long, arduous trip from one coast to the other. The family settled in Sacramento where a daughter, named after her mother, was born. Mrs. Kotzschmar wrote in her biographical sketch that her mother died in 1864, so later, at the age of 12, she was brought back to Portland by an uncle, who was her legal guardian. It was at the "Home Institute," a day and boarding school run by the Misses Prince, located at 52 Free Street, Portland, that Hermann Kotzschmar met his future wife, Mary Ann Torrey. She was enrolled in the day school, and she became one of his piano students there.

Hermann Kotzschmar (1829-1908) came to America from Germany in 1848, and ultimately found his way to Portland, Maine, where he lived out his life. He became the city's leading musician, conductor, composer and music teacher.

Until her marriage in 1872 Mary Ann Torrey lived with the three Waite sisters, Lucretia Ann (1824-1913), Frances (1827-1901) and Mary Emma (1836-1900), all spinsters, who worked in the retail dry goods trade. In fact, Mary Ann lived with or at least on the same property with the Waite sisters until 1913, when the last of the three sisters, Lucretia, died. They are buried in their family plot in the Old Eastern Cemetery on Congress Street in Portland. On that same plot is a simple, flat stone marking the resting place of Mrs. Kotzschmar.

I suspect that Mary Ann and the Waite sisters were related in some way, but so far I have been unable to find any direct evidence of this.

In 1869 Mary Ann Torrey was the youngest of the 35 charter members of Portland's Rossini Club, the oldest continuing woman's musical organization in the United States. Rossini Club records show that Miss Torrey was a very active member, performing often—sometimes two or three times a month—on Rossini Club weekly recitals. Minutes of the group show that in 1871 and '72 Miss Torrey sometimes appeared as a duet partner, teaming up with guest artist Hermann Kotzschmar. There is a record of a spring evening recital when Miss Torrey performed and Mr. Kotzschmar was one of the ushers. It is only in Rossini Club records that she is referred to by her maiden name, and her married name is in parenthesis.

The Kotzschmars had two children, Hermann Jr., born in 1874, and Dorothea, born in 1878. In 1938, the year after his mother died, Hermann Kotzschmar Jr. was interviewed by a Portland newspaper. He is quoted as saying that his father had wanted to return to his homeland, Germany, in the years at the end of the 19th century. Although the elder Kotzschmar had become a naturalized United States citizen on May 29, 1855, he ultimately decided against foreign travel at that time because of prevailing political unrest and conflicts in the world. Therefore, in 1897 Hermann Kotzschmar chose to stay at home in Portland while his wife and daughter traveled abroad.

It was not easy, however, for Mrs. Kotzschmar to leave her husband and son behind for such a long period of time, and in fact she alludes to this in her very first letter *(Page 2)*. And she may have had butterflies in her stomach, remembering her last extended trip when, 33 years earlier, at the age of 12, she was brought to Maine from Sacramento, California either overland or by sea.

Hermann Kotzschmar never returned to the land of his birth. In light of this fact, Mrs. Kotzschmar's visit to the town in Germany where her husband was born *(Page 232)* must have been very significant. Why then, did Dorothea not accompany her mother to visit their relatives there? Dorothea Kotzschmar was fluent in German, and the communication/translation problem would have been easily solved had she been on hand. It may be that she was actually studying German (possibly in Berlin) and in fact a handwritten note on her transcript from Smith College reads: "Work done in German, excused from Junior group in view of philosophy electives." This trip did

happen just before her third year in college, and Dorothea mad several trips to Germany in ensuing years. She studied at the University in Berlin during the summers of 1900, 1902 and 1904, married a Dresden native, Arthur Sachsee, in 1906 and settled with him in New York, where she became the Head of the German Department at Hunter College High School.

I have located photographs of Dorothea Kotzschmar in the archives at Smith College; one of these images has been kindly lent to me for the cover image. It was taken in 1899, two years after this trip, but it seems very appropriate for this book, as much of the land travel for sightseeing that Dorothea and her mother did was by horse-drawn conveyances.

I deeply regret that I can find no photograph of Mrs. Mary Ann Kotzschmar, though I have looked far and wide and even advertised in newspapers and periodicals. I will be absolutely delighted if the publication of this book actually produces her likeness from some "stone left unturned."

Both of the Kotzschmar children married, but there were no grandchildren. (Dorothea died of heart disease in 1931, and Hermann, Jr. died of liver disease in 1945.) I am therefore left to form in my mind a sense of Mrs. Kotzschmar's character and personality through some knowledge of her personal history and the writings she has left behind.

In the last years of the 19th century Mrs. Kotzschmar presented a lecture series in Portland and at other Maine venues. Titled "Outline of the Growth of Music, from A.D. 1000 to A.D. 1850," they were given locally at Kotzschmar

Hall and received fine reviews. Each presentation included musical illustrations by her husband and other prominent area musicians. In 1907 Mrs. Kotzschmar wrote a book about teaching music to young children. She also wrote various short articles and stories in the early years of the 20th century for *The Etude* magazine, *The Ladies' Home Journal*, and *Kosmos*, a small magazine of women's writings, published in 1910. As you will find in this book, she wrote with charm and crispness, obviously enjoying her craft.

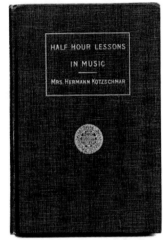

Mary Ann Torrey Kotzschmar was a woman of strong convictions, pure impulses, well-honed passions, and kind regard for her fellow human beings. She was intelligent and refreshingly creative. She had a good sense of humor, as well as boundless energy and enthusiasm for life. She loved children, and excelled at teaching them music, both individually and in class lessons. She was very keen about knowing what the latest trends in teaching methods were, and she kept abreast of new innovations through reading and study with master teachers and performers in larger cities.

I have extracted portions of Mrs. Kotzschmar's descriptions about her trip and illustrated them mainly with vintage postcards of the era. I have used postcards because there are no photographic remembrances of the trip that I could find,

although in her travel letters she twice mentioned someone in the group using a Kodak camera. Postcards came into vogue in the last quarter of the 19th century, and could very well have been used by Mrs. Kotzschmar to send personal messages back to her family and friends in the states. Therefore, they seem a very appropriate form of illustration in this instance.

Whenever possible, I have deliberately selected cards that come from the period 1895 until 1910. Most early postcards provided no space for a written message, so many times the sender would jot a few lines on the picture side of the card. The reader will notice several examples of this in the book.

Also, the charming wildflowers used on the dedication page, Page 224 and on the back cover, were found pressed into the 1897 Baedeker's *Guide to Great Britain*, one of the several Baedekers which I used for reference.

I have allowed the writer's voice to do the narrating, though I have occasionally added a short explanation or clarification (in italics) to help the recounting of the journey, but basically this is Mrs. Kotzschmar's sharing of her travels, observations, opinions and thoughts with us. She did not waste time, so let us get on with her story....

JANICE PARKINSON-TUCKER
Archivist, Friends of the Kotzschmar Organ
Portland, Maine
October, 2004

xv

Collections of Mystic Seaport Archives

*The **S. S. Parisian** was the first large steamer built for the Allan Line by R. Napier & Sons, of Glasgow, and was launched in November of 1880. She was the first to have bilge keels to dampen the rolling, thus reducing seasickness. The ship was of steel construction with screw propulsion, straight bow, and four masts; there were accommodations for 150 first class, 100 second class, and 1,000 third class passengers. In 1902 the **Parisian** was equipped with the first wireless. In April 1912, the ship helped rescue some **Titanic** survivors. The ship sailed for three decades between Liverpool, Canada and the United States, and was scrapped in Italy in January of 1914.*

"A Portland Party's Trip Across the Atlantic"

"Have our dreams indeed become reality and are we actually going to Europe!" exclaimed E, with breathless delight.

❨ *Thus Mrs. Hermann Kotzschmar opens her travel letters back home to the **Portland Daily Press.** As she "sets the scene" for her newspaper readers, she explains her shorthand reference method for herself and daughter Dorothea, to be used throughout her letters.*

1

Before writing further, we wish to explain our use of the first person plural. It is by no means the conventional editorial "we" but a bone-fide one consisting of two distinct individualities. W the elder, E the younger uniting such perfect sympathy in tastes and mutual comprehension, that for us it is an ideal "WE" who are to see together the wonder and the glory of the Old World.

Besides this close personal "WE," to speak with the mathematical exactness of the immortal Wordsworth, "We are eight." The Portland papers have made such slight reference to our party, that for the benefit of those who may have missed seeing the occasional notice, we will particularize our numbers: Monsieur, Madame and Mademoiselle, The Traveler, and close beside her Miss Dot, Mrs. Tapley (a cousin of Mark determined to make the best of everything) and "WE."

W   E

Collections of Smith College Archives

THOSE WHO HAVE EXPERIENCED the stir and excitement of "getting ready" will understand what the few days preceding the sailing of the *Parisian* meant to us, the deciding of the momentous question, what to take, what not to take, the struggle to induce a fair sized trunkful, to compress itself into small enough space to make a respectable looking "hold-all."...

And yet through all those dear delightful days, we kept having such strange sensations in our throats. We were told later that such sensations always come when two go, and two are left behind.

The day so long expected, the 8th of April *(1897)* dawned through cloudy skies, but we were confident the heavens would give us a smiling goodbye and sure enough when on board and ready to start, the sun was shining brilliantly—at least we think it was—perhaps it was the cordial good wishes that made everything look so sunny, surely the one event most delightful to experience in one's life—next to being married—is to leave Portland on the S.S. *Parisian* for a European trip of six months.

☾ *"...when two go, and two are left behind"* —*Mrs. Kotzschmar and daughter Dorothea are travelling, while husband Hermann and son Hermann, Jr. will be staying behind.*

The Old Town Clock, Halifax, N. S.

HALIFAX

FROM THURSDAY EVENING, after leaving Portland, until the following Tuesday, thick fog, alternating with rain and snow, was our pattern. When we reached Halifax, Nova Scotia, the streets and houses were covered with snow.

Whatever beauties Halifax may possess in summer, they are not in evidence in April, but the rain falling on limp fish, withered cabbages and the like, did not induce us to linger long. In three hours we became sufficiently acquainted with Halifax, and returned to the steamship amusing ourselves with watching the various new-comers.

At four o'clock, amid hand-shaking and handkerchief-waving, the *Parisian* weighed anchor; once more we started; land was soon left behind and for the first time we realized that we were "afar and afar on an ocean."

☾ …"afar and afar on an ocean" are the first two lines of a duet between Faust and Margherita in the opera **Mefistofele**, composed by Arrigo Boito (1842-1918). The opera premiered at La Scala on March 5, 1868. Boito was known during his lifetime as a poet and a librettist, as well as a composer. He was the librettist for Verdi's operas **Otello** and **Falstaff**.

At Sea

It is a week today since we left home, and while since Monday we have had pleasant sunny days, yet the captain tells us there is more rolling motion to the ship than he has experienced for two years, except during storms; probably owing to the way in which the freight is stored. People have much to say about the restfulness of an ocean voyage, but to us it is exasperating to the nerves, whatever it may be to the body. We want to be able to calculate upon ourselves with a reasonable degree of certainty, and if we choose a sitting posture not to be made to stand, willy nilly, by a downward dip of the deck. Or if we think we would like a short walk, be compelled to sit in a humiliating heap. We are confident St. Paul must have had one of his many voyages in mind when he wrote, "the things that I would I do not, and the things that I would not, these I do."*

* Romans 7:15

❨ *The voyage continued; Good Friday was observed with a religious service at sea.*

    "Travel" to use the language of our childhood's copy-book, broadens the mind and increases the power of observation, but little did we dream that the actual sensations and experiences of the early navigators would be ours, but now we know precisely the feelings with which "in fourteen hundred ninety two, Columbus crossed the ocean blue." Have we not had mutiny on board, in our own mental conditions, and when late Saturday night we saw stray potato-parings floating on the sea, and heard in the distance the cheerful (to us) grunting of homely but familiar animals, we knew land was near which we immediately christened "Ireland," mentally pressing our lips to dear, steady Mother Earth and exultingly waving aloft our ensign, a hand bag. Soon the rugged coast of the Emerald Isle was outlined across the sky. With what eagerness we gazed at the different peaks and rough rocks, over which dashed the most vivid green water we have ever seen.

Moville Co. Donegal

IRELAND

THE *Parisian* ANCHORED A SHORT DISTANCE from Moville, a small village of two or three hundred houses, twelve miles from Londonderry. Only a short stay was made, long enough to allow the tug to bring and take back the mails. We were delighted to have our first glimpse of Irish gorse, a small prickly shrub covered with bright yellow flowers. It grows on the rocks and the sides of the hills and adds greatly to the attractiveness of the landscape.

☾ *Gorse is a very spiny and dense evergreen shrub, common throughout Western Europe. It is well-suited to maritime climates and coastal areas.*

Baedeker's GREAT BRITAIN.

Landing Stage & S.S. Baltic, Liverpool.

LIVERPOOL.
1:14.500

"IN MERRIE ENGLAND:" LIVERPOOL

"LADIES, IT IS 5:30, the rising bell will ring immediately. We are at Liverpool and breakfast will be served at 6:30." All this was said on Easter Monday morning by the obliging stewardess on the *Parisian*, in a voice which blended encouragement, persuasiveness and command, in a way wholly indescribable. But "what was Liverpool to us or we to Liverpool!"

The ship was steady, and sleep the one thing desirable; but in a waking doze, we realized that shortly after seven the steamer would move to her own dock, so we made a hasty toilet, and still more hasty breakfast, and prepared for the grand scramble of baggage claiming and inspection.

All our traps were in our stateroom marked with a big, big K. It takes time and patience to drag out one's belongings, and the earnest, appealing way to which we denied having cigars, tobacco or perfumery must have touched the inspector's heart, for he simply unlocked the steamer-trunk, lifted the tray, which he at once replaced, and obligingly relocked the trunk, not even opening our bags.

Mr. and Mrs. H, friends of one of our party, met us with the greatest cordiality and showed us the sights, the first of course being the docks, for which we took the elevated electrics, riding north and south by seven miles of dock, and forty of anchorage, something one can see nowhere but in Liverpool.

We had intentionally left our "rush" in Portland, and were sauntering along with what we considered proper English repose. Suddenly the electric began to move, and we were left on the platform. Mr. H. remonstrated with the guard, and we were surprised to hear him say "hurry up," but it did sound homelike.

9

10

Easter Monday is Bank Holiday, and also "Primrose Day." Beaconsfield's statue, fronting St. George's Hall, was covered from the base of the pedestal nearly to the top; wreaths and shields with appropriate inscriptions being sent by different societies; while every man, woman and child we met wore a bunch of the bright blossoms.

When we attempted to see the interior of St. George's Hall we were told it was closed to the public. "We have only one day in Liverpool, and have just come from America," we cried in chorus. "Under those circumstances &c" was the courteous response, and in we went.

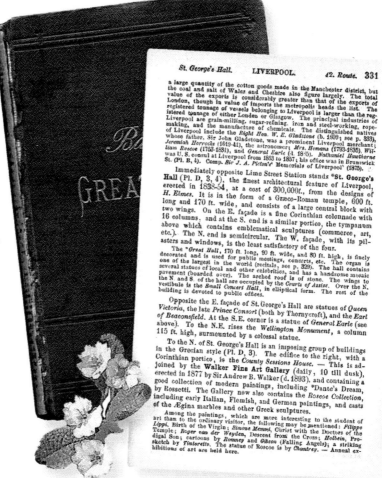

a large quantity of the cotton goods made in the Manchester district, but the coal and salt of Wales and Cheshire also figure largely. The total value of the exports is considerably greater than that of the exports of London, though in value of imports the metropolis heads the list. The registered tonnage of vessels belonging to Liverpool is larger than the registered tonnage of either London or Glasgow. The principal industries of Liverpool are grain-milling, sugar-refining, iron and steel-working, rope-making, and the manufacture of chemicals. The distinguished natives of Liverpool include the *Right Hon. W. E. Gladstone* (b. 1809; see p. 333), whose father, Sir John Gladstone, was a prominent Liverpool merchant; *Jeremiah Horrocks* (1619-41), the astronomer; *Mrs. Hemans* (1793-1835), *William Roscoe* (1753-1831), and *General Earle* (d. 1885). *Nathaniel Hawthorne* was U.S. consul at Liverpool from 1853 to 1857; his office was in Brunswick St. (Pl. B, 4). Comp. *Sir J. A. Picton's* 'Memorials of Liverpool' (1875).

Immediately opposite Lime Street Station stands *St. George's Hall* (Pl. D, 3, 4), the finest architectural feature of Liverpool, erected in 1838-54, at a cost of 300,000l., from the designs of *H. Elmes.* It is in the form of a Græco-Roman temple, 600 ft. long and 170 ft. wide, and consists of a large central block with two wings. On the E. façade is a fine Corinthian colonnade with 16 columns, and at the S. end is a similar portico, the tympanum above which contains emblematical sculptures (commerce, art, etc.). The N. end is semicircular. The W. façade, with its pilasters and windows, is the least satisfactory of the four. The *Great Hall,* 170 ft. long, 90 ft. wide, and 80 ft. high, is finely decorated and is used for public meetings, concerts, etc. The organ is one of the largest in the world (recitals, see p. 329). The hall contains several statues of local and other celebrities, and has a handsome mosaic pavement (boarded over). The arched roof is of stone. The wings to the N. and S. of the hall are occupied by the *Courts of Assize.* Over the N. vestibule is the *Small Concert Hall,* in elliptical form. The rest of the building is devoted to public offices.

Opposite the E. façade of St. George's Hall are statues of *Queen Victoria,* the late *Prince Consort* (both by Thornycroft), and the *Earl of Beaconsfield.* At the S.E. corner is a statue of *General Earle* (see above). To the N.E. rises the *Wellington Monument,* a column 115 ft. high, surmounted by a colossal statue.

To the N. of St. George's Hall is an imposing group of buildings in the Grecian style (Pl. D, 3). The edifice to the right, with a Corinthian portico, is the *County Sessions House.* — This is adjoined by the **Walker Fine Art Gallery** (daily, 10 till dusk), erected in 1877 by Sir Andrew B. Walker (d. 1893), and containing a good collection of modern paintings, including *Dante's Dream,* by Rossetti. The Gallery now also contains the *Roscoe Collection,* including early Italian, Flemish, and German paintings, and casts of the Ægina marbles and other Greek sculptures.

Among the paintings, which are more interesting to the student of art than to the ordinary visitor, the following may be mentioned: *Filippo Lippi,* Birth of the Virgin; *Simone Memmi,* Christ with the Doctors of the Temple; *Roger van der Weyden,* Descent from the Cross; *Holbein,* Prodigal Son; cartoons by *Romney* and *Gibson* (Falling Angels); a striking sketch by *Tintoretto.* The statue of Roscoe is by *Chantrey.* — Annual exhibitions of art are held here.

11

12

A London Omnibus.

IT WAS A NOVEL EXPERIENCE to mount the narrow steps that lead to the top of the trams (primitive looking horse cars), but the sights one sees from this elevation are far more interesting than those obtained in a carriage drive.

Two street gamin, recognizing at once that we were daughters of "Uncle Sam," followed the tram, turning summersaults and hand-springs, hoping for a "ha-penny."

❆ *The ha-penny, or half penny, was a negotiable English coin from about 1816 until 1971. It is often referred to in children's literature and verse; as, for example, in the song*

> *Christmas is coming, the goose is getting fat,*
> *Please to put a penny in the old man's hat.*
> *If you haven't got a penny, a ha'penny will do,*
> *If you haven't got a ha'penny, then God bless you.*

Chester

☾ *On Easter Monday April 19, 1897, at 2:15 p.m., the group left Liverpool for Chester. They went by train to "the most ancient of England's cities."*

After a short rest at the Grosvenor Hotel, they attended the 4:15 Choral Service at Chester Cathedral. The Chancel was beautifully decorated with spring flowers, and before the service the travelers read many of the burial tablets on the walls of the Cathedral.

14

GROSVENOR HOTEL, CHESTER

THE EAST GATE, CHESTER.

CHESTER. EASTGATE STREET, AND THE EASTGATE.

15

THERE CERTAINLY IS a never to be forgotten sensation on entering for the first time an English Cathedral; and when the first is also one of the oldest it brings to mind many a forgotten bit of history.

The Choir, Chester Cathedral

THE CITY WALL, CHESTER

TUESDAY MORNING we took the most memorable walk of our lives. It is not an every day experience to stand on a foundation laid nearly two thousand years ago, and look on the same land and sky on which "great Caesar" gazed. Nearly opposite the Grosvenor Hotel are a set of worn steps leading to the city wall, and the two miles around the wall are crowded with interesting sights. This wall must be an incentive to people to keep their backyards "swept and garnished," for with few exceptions they were exquisitely neat and pretty; with trim flower beds and English ivy covering the houses on whose tops are countless chimney pots.

18

PLATFORM N°1.

N°2 PLATFORM N°

TELEGRAPH
OFFICE

Paddington Station.

In Transit

Arriving in London by dark was the day's ultimate goal, but along the way the band of intrepid Maine travelers missed no opportunity for sight seeing. Early in the day they took a small steamer up the River Dee to Eaton Hall. During the day the weather suddenly turned unpleasant.

WE HAD OFTEN HEARD that it rained easily in England, but such a gentle, persistent, never let go rain was totally different from our aggressive American rains. You realized that although it might cease for a moment it would soon begin again, and continue till the last drop was down. In such a rain we visited Hawarden Castle. From the carriage window we noticed a fallen tree—it was not labeled "felled by Mr. Gladstone" * —everything was too wet to be attractive. The lambs shivered, the cows looked disconsolate, and we wrote in our notebook, "Do not go sight seeing in the rain."

The group decided to delay leaving Oxford for ninety minutes, and used the time to hire a hansom cab in order to catch a fleeting glimpse of the twenty-five colleges and chapels there. They promised themselves a longer visit in May—

'Twas but a fleeting glimpse of Old Oxford, but it was wonderful.

The train engine started, we flew by miles and miles of hedges, so velvety in appearance that we felt as if our hands would sink far down in their plush-like smoothness. We saw in the distance spires innumerable. The twilight fell, the lights began to glimmer thicker and faster. One thought filled our mind—our dream of years was to become a fact.

The guard opened the door of the compartment, and with a long drawn breath of inexpressible delight we cried, "We are in London!"

William Ewart Gladstone (1809-1898) was a great Victorian statesman who served his country as Prime Minister four times. He was a colorful person with several diverse hobbies and passions, one of them being chopping down trees!

"Kotzschmar Party in London"

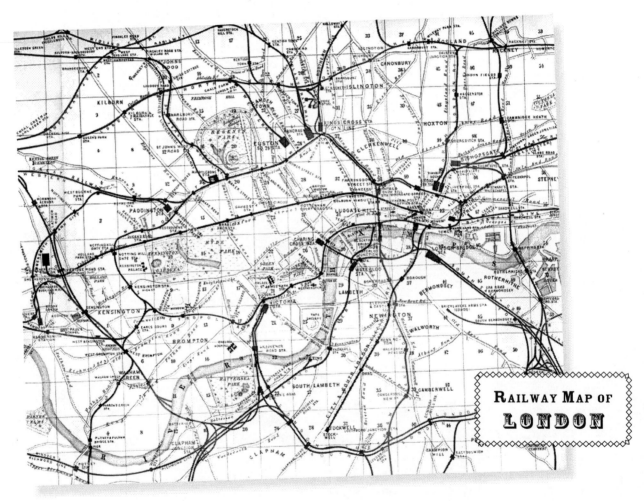

20

RAILWAY MAP OF
LONDON

PICCADILLY, LONDON.

☾ *On their first morning in London the travelers were fortunate to engage a set of rooms at 5, St. Ann's Terrace, for their three month stay. They were near shops, so they could buy fresh food to prepare, and near a tube (underground) station for their sightseeing adventures. All was well!*

The Strand and Charing Cross, London

"TAKING IN THE SIGHTS AND SOUNDS OF THE GREAT CITY"

LONDON FROM THE TOP OF A BUS! There is nothing comparable to it, and if a seat can be secured directly back of the driver one needs no Baedecker [sic]. We started from Charing Cross one sunny afternoon for our first drive.

❦ *Karl Baedeker (1801-1859), son of a German book printer, started his own publishing company in 1827 in Koblenz. It was there that he published the first of his many travel guides—the little red books that became famous for their detailed and accurate information and maps. The term "Baedeker" became synonymous with the best of guidebooks for tourists. A traveler's "Baedeker" could absolutely be trusted as a companion because it contained the most up-to-date descriptions and history of all that was important to see and do in a given country or area of the world. The books were available in several languages. After Karl's death, his third son, Fritz, took over the company. The Baedeker guides are still popular today.*

24

LONDON,—TRAFALGAR SQUARE.

AFTER WE HAD LOOKED LONG at famous Trafalgar Square, guarded by the four immense lions, the two fountains sending up great columns of water, the beautiful National Gallery at the back—

"Of what does it all remind you?" queried E,

"The World's Fair at Chicago!" we cried promptly.

"Think of being on the Strand in London," exclaimed Mrs. Tapley. "I have been pinching myself all the way and saying "Am I, or am I not I!"

We left our first 'bus at the Bank of England and later took another for our first view of the Houses of Parliament and Westminster.

We are perfectly conscious of our limitations so made a vow before leaving home that we would not attempt description, knowing what a failure it would prove, but what we omit in length and breadth, we shall endeavor to supply in personal sensations.

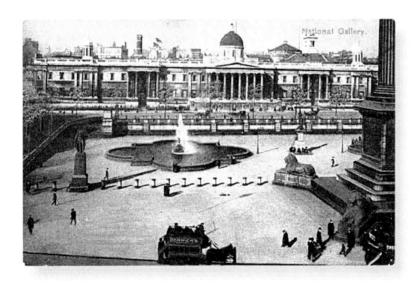

As we gazed at these magnificent buildings, we realized as never before the youth, the newness of America. No pictures, no words can give an adequate impression of them, and it is only as we look, and return to look again and again, that we can faintly appreciate their antiquity, and the wondrous meaning of it all begins to dawn upon us.

The British Museum, London.

ALMOST THE FIRST THINGS we looked at in the British Museum were the manuscripts of Haydn, Mozart and Beethoven; to us, these naturally meant more than the "Elgin Marbles" though before us were the carvings of Phidias; but we have yet to describe the most enjoyable experience we have had since we left home, the memory of which will remain as long as we live.

☾ *The Elgin Marbles were the work of Phidias, the most prominent Greek sculptor, who did original work on the Parthenon. The sculptures are now in London, but there is a movement to return them to their original site.*

MUSICAL  LONDON

BEFORE LEAVING PORTLAND we said "We have presentiment that the first oratorio we hear in London will be Felix Mendelssohn's *Elijah*." We were laughed at, but nevertheless the conviction remained. It is an easy matter to imagine with what exultation we read the following placard as we left the Museum on Sunday afternoon:

> Elijah to be given at Queen's Hall
> Sunday April 25th
> doors open at 6:30, performance begins at 7

In less time than it takes to write it, two of us had started for Queen's Hall, the remainder of the party having other engagements.

The national "Sunday League Musical Society" of which Sir Arthur Sullivan is president, is certainly doing practical Christian work by furnishing Sunday evening entertainments to working people. Once a week, oratorios and other famous works of the greatest composers are given by a chorus of 320 voices, and an orchestra of 50 men; the solo parts are sustained by a double quartette of London's leading singers. Admission is free to certain parts of the house, while to others 6d is charged. These latter seats are in every way desirable and the music is heard to the best advantage.

It was rather unusual to look over the score of *Elijah* with a young girl of fourteen—evidently of the middle class—who showed by her manner and enthusiastic applause that she was familiar with the music, and deeply touched by it; but it is scarcely possible to conceive of anyone who would not be thrilled by this most dramatic of all oratorios.

The part of *Elijah*, sung by Mr. Douglas Powell, was most expressively rendered. The chorus was well balanced, the quality of the voices, especially the sopranos, was very beautiful. The attacks were excellent and the Baal choruses electrifying, chills chasing each other up and down our backs as we listened; but the appealing cry—*"Help! Send thy people help, oh! God!"* completely unnerved us; we pressed each other's hands and the tears would not stay back. For both of us it was an evening of the purest enjoyment; before we realized it the last chorus was sung, and we were hurrying forth for our 'bus.

THE ZOO

WHO IS GOING TO THE ZOO? Was the question asked at the breakfast table Monday morning. Seven hands were instantly raised and preparations were soon made.

"You can easily walk, it is only a step," smilingly spoke our landlady. Little did we realize the length of an English step! Like henny-penny "we goed and we goed" till we met a fox in the guise of a policeman.

"How much farther to the Zoo?" we asked, ready to drop with fatigue. "Only a step," was the reply. But we were wise now, and with knowing look we hailed a 'bus, seated ourselves with a long drawn sigh of satisfaction when lo! We were at the Zoo!

❰ *This London bobby (left) is Sergeant Herbert Frederick Earl, who joined the metropolitan police in 1896 and worked until his pension in 1921. He was awarded the Queen Victoria Diamond Jubilee medal, Edward VII coronation medal and George V coronation medal.*

London — "The Zoo"

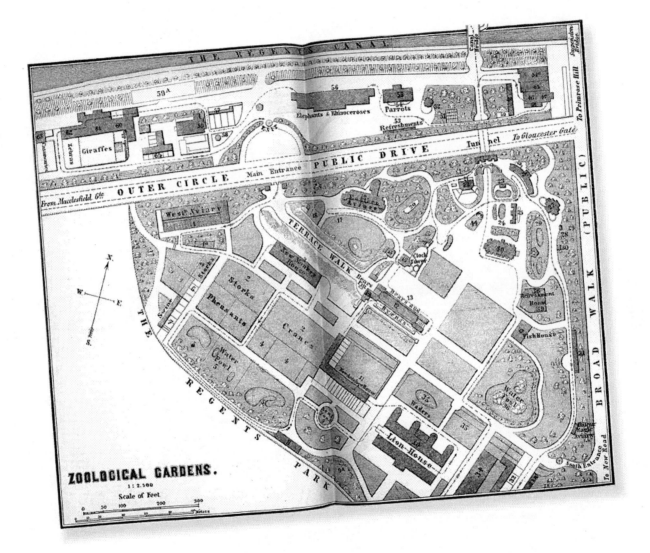

THE REGENT'S CANAL.

59A

56

Elephants & Rhinoceroses

Parrots

53

Refreshments

To Primrose Hill

To Gloucester Gate

Tunnel

Zebras

Giraffes

OUTER CIRCLE

From Macclesfield Gte

Main Entrance   PUBLIC   DRIVE

West. Aviary

TERRACE WALK

Lion Tower

New Monkey House

Storks

Clock Tower

BROAD   WALK   (PUBLIC)

Bears and

Storks

Bear Pit

Pheasants

Cranes

Hyena

Fish House

Water Fowl

Waders

Refreshment House 39I

The   REGENT'S   PARK

Lion House

Water Fowl

South Entrance

To New Road

ZOOLOGICAL GARDENS.

1 : 2.500

Scale of Feet

0   50   100   200   300

Metres

30

Down we clambered, feeling foolish, and with a sense of kinship went first to look at the geese. We found the kangaroos particularly interesting; one immense fellow, whose keeper had brought him up on the bottle, could not be restrained from showing his affection; whenever the man came near him, he would leap upon him like a dog, lapping his face and giving every evidence of fondness. The baby kangaroos kept playing hide and seek, darting in and out of the pouch-like beds where the mother carries her young; their bright beady eyes and sharp pointed noses gave them the appearance of young foxes, as they poked their heads out of the pouch. But the gambols of the kangaroos, the antics of the monkeys, were not to be compared to the fascinations of the giraffe. We stumbled upon his abode by accident, and at first thought it tenantless, but soon perceived "his highness" peering at us from the sky light. Complacently he gazed down at us, one by one, as if to measure our height.

THE ZOO. (London). - The Bear

31

"London Fogs!"—The English Clime

NOT THE LEAST OF THE ATTRACTIONS OF THE ZOO are the flower beds gorgeous with spring blossoms; the green grass, the beautiful shrubs and trees that are everywhere present in England.

We can hardly accustom ourselves to this universal verdure; every tiny house has a bit of green growing about it somewhere, if it is only a small window garden. By why shouldn't England be a vast garden? The sky is an immense watering pot; you never stir without umbrella and "gums." You place not the least dependence upon a smiling sun, for you know that somewhere behind him lurks a big cloud that only waits for you to don best bib and tucker in order to try to give you a drenching!

CERTAINLY LONDON MEANS TO GIVE US a specimen of all sorts of weather, for we have seen a real November fog, so our 'bus driver informed us as we were driving down Regent Street. We shall surely recognize it the next time, without an introduction; it wrapped us round in its yellowish, smoky atmosphere; it shut everything from our sight but the 'bus next in front of us; we knew there were "hundreds to right of us, hundreds to left of us" but not one could we see. We might easily have imagined ourselves in some vast wilderness, but that suddenly high through the mist and fog, high above our heads, on a swinging board, we read the familiar legend "Pears' Soap" and felt then that we still had a grip on things terrestrial. As our 'bus moved carefully along, lights began to gleam from shop windows, although it was only 9:30 in the morning.

Soon the streets were illuminated brilliantly, but by two o'clock the sun was shining as brightly as if there never was, never could be, such a thing as fog. We are told every cause produces an effect; we positively know the effect of a London fog on clothes; said fog is a most remarkable mud producer, and such mud, such extremely muddy mud, we never came in contact with; it is active and impartial beyond expression, and spread itself evenly and thoroughly over both boots and skirts; what small remnant the street left uncovered the 'bus drive home fully finished.

☾ *The phrase "hundreds to right of us, hundreds to left of us" could very well be a paraphrase of lines from Alfred Lord Tennyson's (1809-1893) poem* **Charge of the Light Brigade***, written on April 10, 1864.*

Food and Drink

WHAT READER of Johnson, Goldsmith or Dickens has but resolved on the first visit to England to see a London chop house? We have been consumed from our earliest childhood with an insatiable desire concerning chop houses, pork pie and English puddings. We have now investigated all three. The pork pie we pass over in silence; but the chop house and "ye pudding" we will minutely describe for the benefit of those who may come after us.

Who has not heard of "Ye Old Cheshire Cheese Chop House" at 145 Fleet Street? Imagine four females eagerly scanning each number on Fleet Street one rainy noon in search of the above number. A halt is called before a dingy stairway—but it is not there. Soon we see a dark and gloomy passage that leads we know not where; realizing that "he who hesitates is lost," we enter boldly and are met by one of the pleasantest of English waiters, who politely assures us—"It is all right, Madam, quite right, many ladies come here."

We are ushered into the very room where Dr. Samuel Johnson and his Boswell, with their friends, ate, drank and made merry years ago. It all stands as it has for the past two hundred years—the low ceiling, wainscoting almost reaching to it, high backed benches, long wooden tables, pewter pitchers; over in that corner was Dr. Johnson's favorite seat; there is the very fireplace, the kettle where the time-honored punch was brewed.

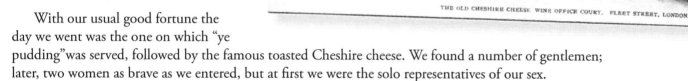

THE OLD CHESHIRE CHEESE, WINE OFFICE COURT, FLEET STREET, LONDON.

35

With our usual good fortune the day we went was the one on which "ye pudding" was served, followed by the famous toasted Cheshire cheese. We found a number of gentlemen; later, two women as brave as we entered, but at first we were the solo representatives of our sex.

"Ye pudding" is always brought in in solemn state and carved by ye host; this has been the custom from the founding of the house. We sat with bated breath and heightened color. In came four men bearing in their arms a pie nearly five feet in circumference; this pie contains beef, mushrooms, lark kidneys and oysters; it is highly seasoned and spiced and covered with a thick crust. After this comes toasted cheese, which is really a Welsh rarebit served in square individual tins, with slices of toasted brown bread. We cannot recall just how it tasted, for we were feasting mentally all the while on Johnson and the great ones who followed him.

We congratulated ourselves on finding this particular chop house, for it is the oldest one in London, its companion in age having been recently torn down to make room for modern buildings.

EMPIRE THEATRE, LEICESTER SQUARE, LONDON.

HIGH JINKS

36

Miss ELLEN TERRY

THE THEATRE

☾ *Mrs. Kotzschmar goes on to talk about the group's theatre experiences; they saw plays at the Haymarket Theatre and the Savoy; at the Lyceum they saw Ellen Terry (1848-1928), the greatest Shakespearian actress of her time and the great aunt of Sir John Gielgud:*

B)UT WHAT ARE THE SAVOY AND HAYMARKET compared to the Lyceum? Ellen Terry as Madame Sans-Gene!* We cannot imagine anything more fetching. In the prologue she is naturalness itself; her costumes as the Duchess are magnificent—white satin embroidered heavily with gold and jewels, and over this a gorgeous court train of deep rose-pink velvet, edged with a broad band of ermine. In the scene with Napoleon (Henry Irving), over the white satin is worn a regal wrap of light green watered silk, lined throughout with ermine, the shoulders trimmed with four ruchings bordered with the same costly fur. The deep Medici collar sets off to advantage the red gold hair and beautiful face of this charming actress. There was not the smallest detail left uncared for; everything was perfection—it was not acting, but reality itself.

The letter ends with a note about the group, which "flies from one form of enjoyment to another, trying to do all the sightseeing possible" because—

Every day the immensity of London grows upon us. Statistics mean but little; one must see it to gain even a faint idea of its vast area. We wish our stay was to be six months instead of three, and with that length of time before us we would not lose a single day in seeing some of the wonderful sights of this "world in itself."

*Mrs. Kotzschmar is referring to a character taken from real life and given the name Madame Sans Gene (Madame without shame) by Victorien Sardou (1831-1908), a French playwright. A simple maid who climbed the social ladder through marriage to a French general during the Napoleonic era, Sans Gene was known for her blunt speech and salty language.

Sunday Best: "London Smartness!"

THE ONE OCCASION AND PLACE to see London style in all its smartness is the Church parade in Hyde Park. We promenaded up and down on Sunday afternoon for several hours till eyes and head were thoroughly weary, viewing the human kaleidoscope. It certainly is a novel sight. The day was pleasant, though cool. (We have nearly perished with the cold since arriving in April.) There must have been thousands of elaborately gotten up women accompanied by the most elegant looking men we every saw. They were all "so near and yet so far" that we felt it was our golden opportunity to look.

It was the first Sunday of the season, and all swelldom was in town. The gowns were as delicate in coloring and trimmed as profusely as one is accustomed to see at teas and receptions. Pearly colored silk poplins, cerise silks under open meshed grenadines; shoulder capes of white watered silk; while the hats were flower gardens of every variety of blossoms in every conceivable color. We specially remarked about the sleeves, tight from wrist to shoulder, where was placed a bow, cap or puff to give a slight fullness; while tailor-made sleeves are invariably a small muttonleg.

"THE KOTZSCHMAR PARTY TOURING THE SHOPS"

IF THERE IS ONE THING more than another that fills the soul of the average woman with satisfaction and self approval it is the consciousness that she has made a complete round of all the shops, that nothing has escaped her observation, not even the latest cut of sleeves, skirt and jacket; and if perchance a bargain is secured then "bliss beyond compare" is hers. We felt when we reached the metropolis that it was a duty we owed to ourselves, our sex and our country to make ourselves familiar with London shops.

"You must surely go to Whiteley's, mustn't you?" said our little landlady, when we were planning our tour of the shops, adding, "It is the largest one in London."

Whiteley's shop is a series of many small shops, one leading into another through archways, of which the most charming is the greenhouse, filled with the largest, sweetest English violets, mammoth mignonette, wonderful orchids, where singing birds and splashing fountains make a picture one cannot forget. The green grocers' department is a dream—such crimson, waxen strawberries of huge proportions we never before knew existed; peaches, pomegranates, pleasant to the eye and taste, at prices suited to the purse of the royal family!

☾ *Whiteley's, opened in Bayswater in 1885, was Great Britain's first department store, and proud to say it could quote a price or offer to buy everything from a pin to an elephant. The store still exists, and was re-modeled in 1989 as a grand mall, with selling space of more than 300,000 square feet.*

Regent Street, London.

☾ *Regent Street and Bond Street are two of the major, up-scale shopping areas in London; both are lined with high-priced and exclusive shops that offer, for example, fine fabrics to be custom-made into suits and ladies' outfits by tailors who measure each customer carefully, hat shops for both sexes, beautiful English-made bone china, sweets, and leather goods.*

LONDON. CHEAPSIDE LOOKING WEST.

EXTREME FROM WHITELEY'S in direction is "Cheapside," something of a misnomer, by the way, many articles being higher priced than on Regent Street. We purchased pens and pencils there, and were obliged to buy the former by the box and the latter by the dozen; but our feelings were soothed and our pride up-lifted, even if our purses were depleted, when the shopkeeper assured us they were the best make in the world—American!

WARDERS OF THE TOWER OF LONDON
THE WARDERS, MORE GENERALLY CALLED "BEEFEATERS" ATTRACT PARTICULAR INTEREST BY REASON OF THEIR UNUSUAL AND PICTURESQUE COSTUME, THE STYLE OF WHICH HAS BEEN RETAINED SINCE THE 16th CENTURY.

42

THE TOWER

POSSIBLY OUR MINDS WERE STILL OVERSHADOWED by the gloom of London Tower. That surely is a gruesome place. We were fortunate to secure as guide a former warden, and if we had implicitly believed his opening address we should have found Mr. Baedeker of '96 but a broken reed to lean upon.

"Now 'ere, ladies," he began "this is Queen Helizabeth riding on 'orseback through the streets of Lunnon, 'haccordin to that'ere guide (casting a withering glance of contempt on the offending red volume) you would have looked on the swords and guns in the h'armory and thought it was 'er; "she's been moved this last year," and proudly and 'aughtily he swept on, followed by a procession of eleven women with six small boys in the rear.

We had no need for Baedeker for guide when we stood in St. John's chapel, and raising our eyes could almost see the shadowy form of William the Conqueror, as he must have stood looking down from the balcony between those Norman pillars that have been here for centuries. What heart but would have thrilled with pity, to see the spot where Anne Boleyn's slender neck paid the penalty for thoughtless vanity and frivolity.

We've seen the Tower once, but those dark dungeons and gloomy winding stairways have witnessed too many deeds of horror to tempt us to go again.

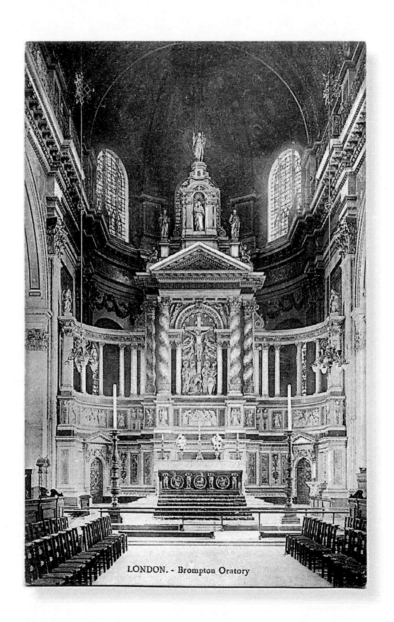

LONDON. - Brompton Oratory

The Brompton Oratory

We **HAD HEARD SO MUCH IN PRAISE** of the music at the Brompton Oratory at South Kensington that we determined to make an early start on Sunday morning and secure a good seat.

The one thing that absorbed us throughout the service was the music; our delight was unspeakable when we heard the first notes of Gounod's most beautiful "Third Mass." It was prayer, praise, sermon —everything in itself. The heavenly Kyrie Eleison! It spoke to our hearts as no human voice alone could do, and as we dropped upon our knees, when the solemn words *"et incarnates est de Spirito et Maria Virgine"* were sung so pianissimo it sounded like a whisper from above— we realized as never before the power of music to touch the human soul.

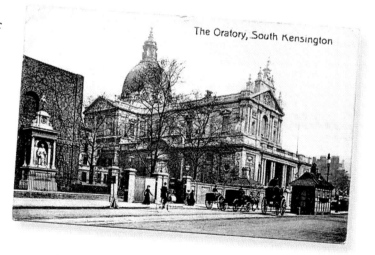

The Oratory, South Kensington

LONDON LOW...

☾ While relating the group's trip to Brompton Oratory, Mrs. Kotzschmar shared her opinion of the London underground:

NO ONE KNOWS what the words dust, dirt and draughts signify until one has traveled underground. Small wonder that the wretched engineers can endure the life only for a few years. Imagine rushing through miles of the darkness of Erebus with only occasional gleams of God's sunlight, as it filters through the windows of the different stations. We raise both hands in favor of the 'bus every time, in spite of occasional unmentionable drawbacks.

46

...AND LONDON HIGH

ONE OF THE GREATEST CHARMS OF LONDON is its endless variety; you start on a commonplace errand, and lo! You are suddenly in the midst of streets and buildings having the most interesting associations.

We planned for a shopping expedition in Cheapside and before we realized it we had forgotten basket-trunks, gloves, all perishable things, and were standing mute and motionless in St. Paul's Cathedral. Its size, its proportions, its ornamentation are so harmonious that we could not at first grasp its grandeur.

We walked through the broad aisles, which unlike Westminster are open, free, not overcrowded with memorials to the dead. We paused before one, whose simplicity satisfied us beyond the others. The open gates, the guardian

LONDON. ST. PAUL'S CATHEDRAL.

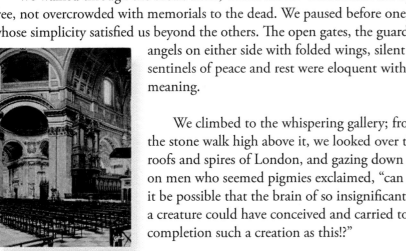

angels on either side with folded wings, silent sentinels of peace and rest were eloquent with meaning.

We climbed to the whispering gallery; from the stone walk high above it, we looked over the roofs and spires of London, and gazing down on men who seemed pigmies exclaimed, "can it be possible that the brain of so insignificant a creature could have conceived and carried to completion such a creation as this!?"

48

"IMPRESSIONS OF VICTORIA REGINA"

THE PORTRAITS OF THE QUEEN are so idealized that one sees no picture of the actual woman. She is far from presenting a queenly figure; imagine a short gray haired person, exceedingly stout, with a round puffy face, glasses on the nose, and dressed in the severest, plainest black—surely nothing could be more unlike one's preconceived notion of a queen, who is supposed to be blessed with perennial youth, loveliness and commanding grace. Victoria in her girlhood is said always to have been photographed standing on a concealed footstool.

THE STATE COACH AND FAMOUS CREAMS.

❮ *The famous cream colored royal horses are of German extraction, originally brought to England from Hanover by King George I (1660-1727). From the beginning of Victoria's reign the creams were bred at Hampton Court, and the horses on this card are descendants of the original group. The creams are unique because of their Roman noses, white muzzles and eyelashes, and are known to create a very handsome display in their royal trappings.*

ROYALTY

W<small>E WERE SO ELATED</small> with our view of the Queen that we determined the following day to try for a glimpse of the Prince and Princess of Wales, as they were to assist at the Queen's drawing room reception.

We started about noon for Buckingham Palace, as all carriages begin to line up as early as one o'clock. The English people, to say nothing of Americans, "dearly love a lord" and for two hours an endless procession filed past the carriages, looking through the open windows at the beauty (?) and fashion of the English aristocracy.

But hurrah! There comes the Princess, and ignorant people, who shall be nameless, began a feeble cheer, which was quickly suppressed as a native Briton rather contemptuously explained "that is a Duchess." But if one sees a brilliant red coach, with gilt trimmings, with two "ilegant gentlemin" in front, and two standing behind, dressed in scarlet coats and gold lace, with white silk stockings, immense shoe-buckles, powdered hair tied in a queue, and red and gold three cornered hats, is it not natural to think that such splendor means a Princess is approaching?

All things come to the women who wait, and soon were seen the outriders—which now we realize always precede royalty—and the lovely Alexandra (powdered, painted and wigged to resemble a girl of twenty) drove by, bowing right and left.

☽ *Alexandra (1844-1925), eldest daughter of King Kristian IX of Denmark, married Edward (1841-1910), son of Queen Victoria and Prince Albert, in 1863. She had six children, including George V, who ascended to the throne when his father passed away in 1910. Her engaging personality and lack of pretense made her a favorite of her mother-in-law, and she was also well-liked by the British people.*

52

The Crystal Palace

BY NO MEANS was the least of our royal experiences the royal welcome we received from Mr. and Mrs. George Moore, soon after our arrival. We are indebted to their cordial hospitality for our first visit to Crystal Palace.

Their delightful home in Upper Norwood, London, combines the elegance of English life with the distinctive home comforts of New England. It was there where we met the genial artist, Mr. Harry Brown, who gave us a hearty greeting, and what a good time we had talking of old friends and familiar scenes!

After a most delicious lunch, we spent several hours in the immense glass palace, whose wonders would take days to see. It being Saturday one attraction was a concert given by four thousand children, the Duke and Duchess of Cambridge being present and distributing prizes to schools having the best record in the study of music. It was an impressive sight to see so vast a number of children, but we were disappointed in the volume of sound, which was far less than we expected.

54

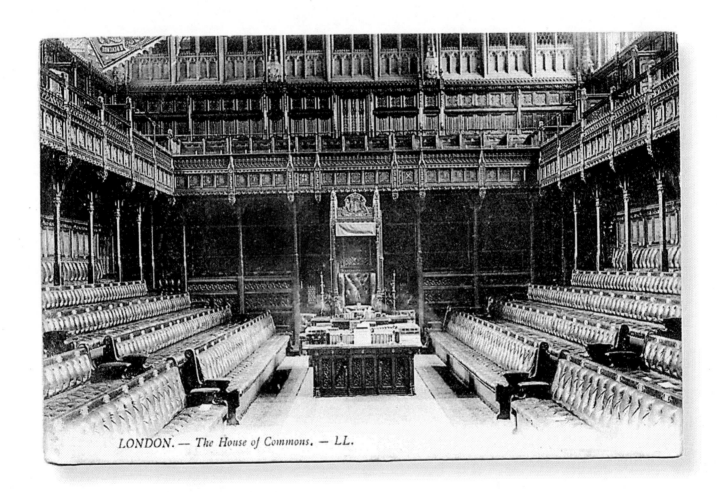

LONDON. — The House of Commons. — LL.

AMERICANS AT PARLIAMENT

OUR INTENTIONS were good to be present at a debate in the House of Commons, but in this matter women proposed, and the members disposed, of the tickets by ballot. The seating capacity of the iron cages—high above that august body—is very limited, and friends of the members often wait months for an opportunity of going and even then fail to secure one.

Under those circumstances we were compelled to content ourselves with walking through the rooms of the magnificent Houses of Parliament. As we left the Queen's robing room which is upholstered in plain crimson terry, another party of Americans came in; one foot-sore and weary woman attempted to sit down for a short rest, but a policeman caught her before the (to him) sacreligious act was quite consummated. "Madame!" he gasped in a trembling voice while his face blanched with horror, and his hand shook with agitation—"no one is permitted to be seated in this room," and as the stranger with great dignity withdrew, the guardian of the place said in an awe-struck whisper to a companion, "Did you see her? She was going to sit down!"

If murder had been perpetrated he could hardly have shown more intense feeling. Poor fellow! We suppose he could not grasp the idea inherent in all daughters of Columbia that nothing is too good for free-born Americans.

LONDON'S OTHER SIDE

Ever since reaching London we have been anxious to see something of the Whitechapel district, and learning that Sunday was the most favorable time for a visit to that quarter, our party started a week ago for that wretched place of poverty and crime.

"Petticoat Lane" is conceded to be the meanest portion, and as all the inhabitants are Jews, Sunday is their day for buying and selling. Both sides of the streets were lined with temporary shops, from which a motley collection of articles was sold, from old iron and rusty nails to ice cream and patent medicines. The place swarmed with people. On the edge of the sidewalk a small boy was struggling to get on a pair of old boots; a little farther on a man was critically scanning himself in a hand glass, undecided as to the becomingness of different second hand derbys. Everyone was intent on his or her business, and not the slightest notice was taken of us. Men were crying their wares in loud tones, but the buyers were quiet and orderly.

We did not hear a profane word or see one intoxicated person throughout the entire trip; undoubtedly the many policemen stationed at short intervals had a wholesome effect upon the crowds. Somewhat to our disappointment we did not meet with a single adventure.

Nature Beckons

"Three Sundays already in town" cried one of us on a bright, sunny morning. "Who votes for a fourth in the country?"

The motion was carried unanimously by seven, and we started for Hampstead Heath.

The ride was through a rather uninteresting portion of the city, but the end of the journey amply justified its being undertaken—a wide expanse of country on top of Parliament Hill! Here one gains a glorious view of London with the noble dome of St. Paul's' and beyond are the green fields with flocks of nibbling sheep; graceful elms shading many ponds, and the ever present church spire, which always dominates an English country scene. We wandered down the hillside, through tall meadow grass, past a group of people listening to a socialist speaker; we caught the words "American Democrats" in a tone of seething sarcasm, and quietly hurried by.

THE STALLS, HAMPSTEAD HEATH.
"FOOD AND DRINKS TO SUIT EVERY TASTE FOR ONE PENNY".

60

THE AIR WAS FILLED with the perfume of fruit blossoms and flowers, the sun as warm as in summer.

We strolled slowly through the churchyard and paused a while to meditate on the text "Favor is deceitful and beauty is vain"* suggested to our mind as we read the epitaph on a tombstone, erected by a bereaved husband, "Here lies the once beautiful Eliza." A little further on we come upon the object of our quest—a marble shaft, a grave with close trimmed turf. There we read "George Eliot." We close our eyes to try and shut away the other name and with our mental vision see around the grave invisible forms—Fair Romola the lonely, Dorothea Casaubbon, proud and beautiful Gwendoline, great hearted Maggie, pretty but wretched Hetty, noble Adam Bede, while near them is that tender woman, inspired preacher, ministering angel Dinah—George Eliot's eternal creations. She is "of those immortal dead who live again in minds made better by their presence."

Proverbs 30:30

☾ *George Eliot (1819-1880) was the pseudonym of Mary Ann Evans, a Victorian writer and free thinker, who lived in a time when writing was thought to be an exclusively male profession. This line is from the famous poem* O May I Join the Choir Invisible. *Some other famous works by Eliot are* Adam Bede, Silas Marner, *and* Middlemarch. *Eliot wanted to be buried in Westminster Abbey, but was denied permission, so rests instead at Highgate Cemetery in London.*

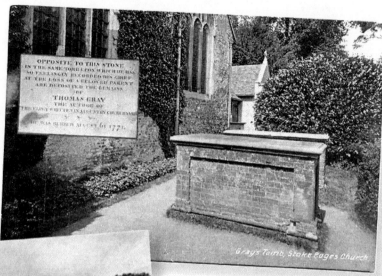

Grays Tomb, Stoke Pages Church

OUR TRIP TO HAMPSTEAD HEATH gave us such a delicious whiff of country air that late the following week we decided that an excursion to Windsor was absolutely essential to our health and happiness. We are so pleased with our newly acquired deliberation of movement that we lose no opportunity to put it in practice, and with such telling effect on the day we started for Windsor, that we reach Paddington Station ten minutes after the express train had left, consequently had half an hour to wait for the accommodation. "How fine," cried Mrs. T. with "Tapley-onian" joviality, "by losing that quick train we can stop on the way and comfortably see Slough and Stoke Poges."

The former is a pretty, though rather sleepy little place, which offers no unusual attraction to a stranger. It is the church yard at Stoke Poges, a drive of two miles from Slough, which attracts all tourists. The day was perfect, the sun bright and warm without being too warm. Our party drove in open landaus through the lovely English country, the road on both sides lined with trees on which the new, tender shoots made a deep fringe of pale green foliage indescribably beautiful while red and white hawthorns filled the air with their sweetness.

63

The calm, the quietness of that country church yard only those can understand who have been there. The verger allowed us to gather some ivy, which grew beneath the spreading yew under whose shade Gray often sat. Close by is the mother's tomb which inspired his deathless poem.

We lingered, reluctant to be gone from such a spot of restfulness and inspiration.

❪ *Thomas Gray (1716-1771) is said to be the finest poetic voice of his age. He is chiefly remembered for his 1751 poem* **Elegy Written in a Country Churchyard,** *said to be the most celebrated poem of its century. It is certainly that poem to which Mrs. Kotzschmar is referring.*

The King at Windsor.

WINDSOR CASTLE FROM THE BRIDGE

WINDSOR

ARRIVING AT WINDSOR, leaving the station and walking a short distance, what was our surprise to see in front of us the towers and battlements of Windsor Castle, and close to its very walls the markets and shops of the town. For some unknown reason we had always pictured to ourselves the Castle as situated in the very centre of Windsor Forest, and completely surrounded by the ancient trees. Consequently, our first sight of it was something of a disappointment, from which we quickly recovered as we viewed the noble structure from a more advantageous point.

"The pomp of power," of which one gains a glimpse in the magnificent state apartments of the Castle, did not impress us half as deeply as standing in the "Old Tower" where the "curfew tolls the knell of parting day," as it did for centuries, though the custom is now discontinued. Formerly the bells were rung whenever the Queen passed to and from the castle, but since the death of the Prince Consort, Albert, they have been silent.

☾ *"curfew tolls the knell of parting day," is the first line of Gray's* **Elegy Written in a Country Churchyard.**

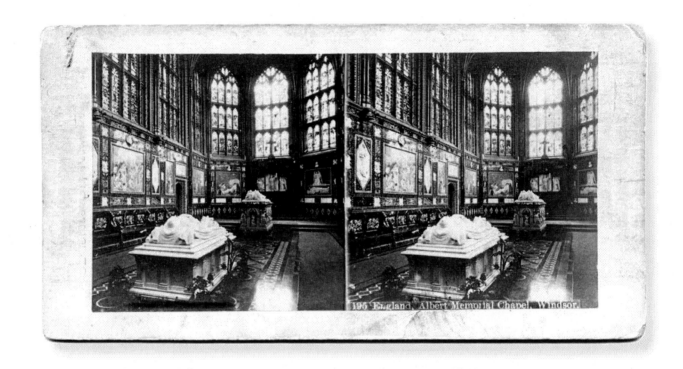

It is only for one day in a year that visitors are allowed to see the tomb of the Prince Consort, but the beautiful Albert Memorial Chapel was open and its decorations are superb.

Windsor Castle, St. George's Chapel, Princess Charlotte

ST. GEORGE'S CHAPEL is filled with most interesting relics of past ages. Here royal children have been baptized, Princes and Princesses joined in marriage, and here mighty kings lie buried.

The one object in the chapel that held us spellbound was the memorial to the Princess Charlotte by whose untimely death at the age of nineteen Victoria inherited the throne. A shrouded figure lies prostrate emblematic of the earthly form of the Princess; hovering above it in the air, seemingly without support, and cut in almost flawless marble, is her glorified body. At the four corners are veiled forms bowed with grief, typifying the world's sorrow at her death.

67

The afternoon sunlight streamed through the stained windows and threw a never-to-be-forgotten glory over the ascending figure.

Collections US Library of Congress

68

1811

COURTESY OF THE US
LIBRARY OF CONGRESS

A
NEW MAP
OF
NORTH AMERICA,
FROM THE
LATEST AUTHORITIES
By JOHN CARY, Engraver.
1811.

HAIL  COLUMBIA

❦ Mrs. Kotzschmar told a wonderful story about gathering the children of the neighborhood where the travelers were staying, to teach them about American geography and way of life.

ON OUR RETURN FROM SIGHT SEEING, a discussion arose in the house (we refer to 5 St. Ann's Terrace) concerning the map of the United States; to strengthen our position, we borrowed an atlas (date 1811) belonging to, and used by, a young girl fresh from her studies. Our bewilderment may be imagined when we found Louisiana extending from Lake Erie along the entire length of the Mississippi River.

But what was that compared to seeing Maine shorn of her E? Then we realized why we were in "darkest England."

Three times a week our mission band collects the heathen from ten years old and upward and lectures are given on Geographical Ethics. "Forget your rising inflection," was our opening address, "neglect to say 'thank you' for nothing, drop your Ls if you will, but never, never drop that final vowel, the inalienable property of Maine, the leading state of America. Rightly does her motto read—'Dirigo!' Does she not lead in statesmen? Are not the greatest singers in verse and music hers? And more than all within her borders is the fairest city in the world—whose streets are beautiful, whose people are the truest, kindest friends on earth; and the name of that city is Portland! Dear old Portland! A million times God bless her!"

*❦ In 1890 William Booth (1829-1919), a religious and social reformer who founded the Salvation Army, wrote **In Darkest England and the Way Out**. In this book Booth outlined a dramatic plan for ending unemployment and overcoming poverty in England.*

70

Epsom Downs

"AT EPSOM DOWNS: THE KOTZSCHMAR PARTY TAKES IN THE RACES"

71

ON LEAVING OUR "NATIVE LAND" the head of the family said, with his parting blessing, "when in England do as the English do;" therefore, with light hearts and "great expectations" we started on June 2nd—Derby Day—for Epsom Downs to see the most famous of English races.

All England went with us, prince and peasant, titled dame and tattered tramp—costers in coats, vests and trousers trimmed with rows of "pearly" buttons; with them their 'Arriets arrayed in "coats of many colors," and hats with at least ten or a dozen waving feathers on each. Near them were charming English girls and "American cousins," all wonderfully gotten up.

This day "all roads led to Epsom."

☾ *A "coster" is a man or woman who sells fruit or vegetables, poultry or fish on the street. In everyday English, it would be a "monger" who "hawks" his wares on the open street.*

LONDON — THAMES EMBANKMENT

72

A Trip Along the Thames

IN ALL LIVES SPECIAL DAYS, certain events forever stand out sharp and distinct amid the succession of weeks and varied incidents of one's experience. Such a red letter day was the Monday "WE" made our first trip on the historic Thames.

For the time being our party had separated, going different ways—this day only W and E were left together to make the journey over waters which recall much of England's story, and whose banks have been the meeting place of men and women famous for all time.

The day, we know, must have been such an one as inspired Lowell to write "What is so rare as a day in June," for nothing could have excelled it in tempered warmth of sunlight, fragrance of blossom, joyous caroling of birds; earth and sky were united in one matchless vision of loveliness. There was not one cloud too many, not one breath of wind too much.

From early morning until late twilight deepened into night—it was a day of days.

ALTHOUGH THE START IS MADE from London Bridge, the picturesque beauty of the Thames is not seen at its best until we reach Kew, whose magnificent gardens we passed their entire length, and where, later, we saw all manner of trees and flowers. From there until we come to the final landing at Hampton Court, one charming scene succeeds another; stately houses surrounded by carefully kept grounds whose fine old trees bend down to the water, and beyond the curve of the river many swans glide by, coming so near us we can almost touch them.

We gain a view of Richmond and of the celebrated "Star and Garter" where Dickens, Thackeray, and scores of other noted men were wont to go in days of Auld Lang Syne; we pass Twickenham and Teddington.

Here for the first time we realized what is meant by a "house boat." The cabin extends along the middle of the boat leaving deck space at either end which is decorated with palms, ferns and flowering plants; here are placed chairs and tables ready for that English custom, as binding as the laws of the Medes and Persians— "afternoon tea." Awnings made in graceful shapes are raised high above the top of the cabin, shielding the upper deck from sun and rain and here are more flowers and singing birds in cages making a veritable earthy paradise; light draperies screen the cabin windows, on the upper deck sat a pretty woman idly holding a piece of fancy work, and beside her the lord of the house boat busily reading.

HAMPTON COURT PALACE.

As we made fast to the pier we discovered that we were at Hampton Court Palace. We saw all its wonders and gazed at Lely's famous court beauties—mentally pooh-poohing—Portland's beauties are so superior! We peeped through the glass door at the one hundred and thirty year old grape vine, loaded with fruit, every bunch of which is sent to Her Majesty.

THE MAZE, HAMPTON COURT PALACE

ENGLISH CURIOS

As Ulysses of old stopped his ears with wax against the voices of the sirens, so we have fortified ourselves against temptation with opaque glasses, shutting out all distractingly alluring objects, are led straightway towards the special curios we wish to see. We thoroughly enjoyed looking at the beautiful Albert Memorial, where a "noble army" of inventors, painters, poets, sculptors and musicians, in chiseled marble surround its four sides, and whose rich coloring and harmonious designs from the long flight of marble steps leading up to it, to the very top of the golden cross which seems to pierce the sky, is certainly a fitting tribute to a wise and noble prince.

117. — LONDON. — *Albert Memorial*

76

OFF THE BEATEN PATH

WE HAVE ACHIEVED ONE BIT OF SIGHT SEEING of which we feel justly proud; one memorable Saturday morning "Dot" and "WE" waked with the lark, also with a neighboring rooster, after making a toilette in a twinkling, and partaking of a barmecide breakfast, we started at 4:30 a.m. for Covent Garden Market.

How still the great city was! How bustling the market place! Our goal was the flower section, in gaining which we passed immense wagons packed solid with radishes, rounded high up, a mass of rosy red. Other carts were similarly filled with turnips in even rows, the green tops alternating with the glistening white of the vegetables; baskets six feet high lined with water cress and countless pyramids of cauliflowers and every known vegetable.

But the flowers made us speechless with delight. There were actually baskets filled with forget-me-nots, lilies of the valley, carnations and roses; mignonette in rows as far as our eyes could see, alternating with huge purple pansies contrasted with golden yellow and pure white. We could well believe it to be the largest flower market in the world. Flower girls jostled us, with baskets five deep filled with flowers, which they were carrying on their heads from carts to stalls, and not one was dropped. The fragrance of that morning lingered with us for days.

❈ *A barmecide breakfast is another of Mrs. Kotzschmar's literary illusions; the term is taken from the* **Arabian Nights** *and refers to a meal that looks good but doesn't live up to expectations.*

78

SCENE IN COVENT GARDEN MARKET

IT WAS IN THE VICINITY OF COVENT GARDEN that we discovered what was formerly the pauper burial ground; the most wretched, forsaken place we have yet seen. Here was the old gateway where Lady Dedlock, in Dickens' *Bleak House*, was found dead; and close by the same miserable hovels where "poor Joe" sometimes lingered till told to "move on."

We have spent days walking through Dickens' London, days filled with a pleasure never before imagined. True, we have often met with disappointments, as when we were told we could surely see the identical house belonging to Sampson Brass and his charming sister, the fair Sally. After hunting for hours and finding the very spot, we saw—only new handsome structures in place of the building so intimately associated with Dick Swiveller

and the Marchioness. We walked miles to see Grip, poor Barnaby Rudge's faithful friend, only to find that he was no longer on exhibition; but were we not recompensed when we saw "The Old Curiosity Shop" where little Nell and her grandfather lived?

It is never wise, on such expeditions, too carefully to enquire as to "hard Gradgrind facts." Accept what is offered and give thanks.

❨ *Thomas Gradgrind is a character in Charles Dickens' novel* **Hard Times.** *Gradgrind was the founder of the Gradgrind educational system, which focused on teaching children cold, hard facts. "Nothing else will ever be of any service to them," he declared.*

We have left London for a time, but the spell is still upon us as we write, and the manifold fascinations of that great city are fresh in our minds.

☾ *Mrs. Kotzschmar went on to describe some of the concerts the Mainers attended: they saw* **Lohengrin** *at Covent Garden Opera House and heard the pianist D'Albert give his final London concert of the season with the London Philharmonic Orchestra, playing his own concerto. She wrote:*

The concert in its entirety was unusually fine—a new suite conducted by the composer Hamish McCann, and Mme. Albani, who sang twice. The closing number, Beethoven's **8th Symphony**, was given with rare taste and expression. It was a concert that made one feel perfectly happy and glad to be alive to listen to such wonderful music.

❮ *In the days preceding Victoria's Jubilee on June 22, Mrs. Kotzschmar and her friends spent time visiting the art exhibit at Guildhall, attending the theatre several times, and more musical concerts, of course.*

THE CROWNING ENJOYMENT of the week was a piano recital by the young Russian pianist Gabrielowitch, who is but 19, and plays most artistically. In appearance he is about medium height with the pallor of countenance indicative of a close student. In compositions like Mendelssohn's "Wedding March," arranged by Liszt, his technique is ample, every note clear and telling and the tempo at which it was played—almost equal to that of Paderewski. In Chopin's "Nocturne" and "Ballade" he showed a sympathetic touch. He undoubtedly has a great future before him if he continues as he has begun.

We are eagerly looking forward to a recital June 19th by Paderewski, and on the following Saturday he plays with the Philharmonic orchestra; the only performances in London for the season. How much the concerts mean to lovers of Paderewski's genius!

CITY HALL-PORTLAND

Evening Jan. 23th—Matinee Jan. 24th.

PADEREWSKI

Evening Tickets—Reserved, $1.50 and $2.00. Matinee—$1.25 and $1.50. Admissions $1.00. On sale or mailed at Ira C. Stockbridge's Music Store, 540 Congress St. Damrosch—Jan. 10th, Master Tyler—Jan. 4th, Faust—Dec. 23th. Half fare and late trains.   de24d6t

❮ *Mrs. Kotzschmar had heard and met Paderewski when he performed in Portland in March of 1892, and again early in 1893. On Tuesday, November 19, 1895, Mr. and Mrs. Kotzschmar had presented "A Paderewski Evening" at Kotzschmar Hall in Portland. Mrs. Kotzschmar read an extended paper she had written about the great pianist, and her husband and assisting musicians illuminated the talk with compositions by Paderewski. This event was presented in anticipation of Paderewski's appearance in Portland, during his third American tour.*

*It is a matter of interest that Paderewski wrote in his autobiography (**The Paderewski Memoirs**) about being at the Queen's Jubilee while in London in June, 1897: "…it was a wonderful sight—of a splendor hardly to be imagined."*

82

LONDON BRIDGE, LONDON.

JUBILEE FEVER: "A PORTLAND WOMAN'S IMPRESSIONS OF THE GREAT SPECTACLE"

WE LEFT PORTLAND with at least one definite idea firmly fixed in our brains and that was that we would see the Queen's Jubilee. We are proud to write that the idea remains in the same fixed state; this assertion would be fraught with deeper meaning to our Maine friends if we could recall the exact number of times we have been assured that we were taking our lives in our hands to make the attempt.

Once only have we quaked and our courage flagged. It was while driving over London Bridge at 6 p.m. to watch the throng of people on their way home from business and work. It was almost a blockade and the number of people seemed beyond calculation. "Will June 22nd be worse than this?" we involuntarily questioned, of no one in particular. The quick ear of our 'bus driver caught the query and turning he answered politely, "Begging your pardon Madam, this is no crowd whatever compared to a Jubilee jam! Wait until as far as you can see in front of you and behind you, your eyes rest on nothing but people, not only the sidewalks but the entire street filled with an almost solid mass of moving men, women and children. Not a single 'bus, hansom, team of any description will be allowed on the street the 21st, 22nd and 23rd of June. You don't know much about London crowds, do you?" Eyeing us critically, he added meditatively "There's sure to be a lot of people killed."

We admit frankly, and are not ashamed of the confession—we shivered—but still clung to the conviction that with courage, prudence and a seat we can see Victoria celebrate her reign of sixty years.

❨ *As the Jubilee celebration approached, the American visitors became more and more anxious for the big day to arrive.*

THE FIRST ACTUAL PERSONAL INTIMATION WE RECEIVED that we were "in the thick of the fray" so to speak, was when on Regent Street Saturday morning, looking for our Atlas 'bus, we read "increased Jubilee fares—one shilling any distance."

As we had been paying "tuppence" (four cents) this meant an increase of twenty cents and it made our pocketbook feel as low in coin as we did in spirit. We recovered, however, when we remembered that our numerous pilgrimages through London were ended and that our seats at the rooms of the London Glove Co., where we go for the procession, could be reached by the underground railway, which remained in status quo as to place and fare.

Monday we felt restless, anxious for the morrow; we spent a large portion of the day dallying with dumb-bells, Indian clubs and sand-bags; not that we dreamed we could displace a London crowd, but we simply wanted to be in our usual health and strength.

❨ *As life changed for women in the 19th century, new energy and attention was focused on female health, both physical and psychological. Magazines published frequent articles about hygiene, diet and exercise. They published pages of exercises for women to do at home, if they could not get to a private exercise club, very popular establishments at that time.*

THE ANNOUNCEMENT TO H.M. QUEEN VICTORIA OF HER ACCESSION TO THE THRONE, JUNE 20th, 1837.

DIAMOND JUBILEE REIGNS SUPREME throughout the United Kingdom, from north to south, from east to west, the blaze of countless bonfires lighted simultaneously at a given signal proclaim jubilee! The very air is literally red, white and blue with jubilee; London is decorated from end to end, festoons of green, garlands of roses, gay colored buntings adorn building after building. The electric devices almost baffle description; mottoes hailing "Victoria our Mother Queen." "We loyal, Thou royal," "Sixty years of unexampled prosperity," are what we read on every side.

"Father," we overheard a child ask "what has Victoria done herself that everyone gives her such great praise?" For a moment an answer seemed beyond the father's power; "Ah well, my son, she has been a very good woman, a very good wife and mother, and a very good Queen, very good indeed," he reiterated, clinging to goodness as if that alone made material greatness.

☾ *The scene above illustrates the early morning of June 20, 1837, when young Princess Victoria (1819-1901) was awakened to be informed that her uncle, King William, had passed away and she was now the reigning monarch.*

THE CHIEF INTEREST, ASIDE FROM ROYALTY, centered in the magnificent troops 50,000 strong, representing Her Majesty's forces. It was indeed a glorious sight. Nearly all were mounted on superb horses. Life Guards, Dragoons, Hussars, Lancers, Colonial troops dazzled the eye with their different uniforms and won admiration by their soldierly bearing.

The Indian Contingent was loudly applauded; as well as the endless Earls, Dukes and Royal Princes. In the fifth carriage, in company with the Spanish and French representatives, rode the United States special Ambassador, Mr. Whitelaw Reid, conspicuous by his black coat, tall silk hat and extremely severe expression of countenance.

There were seventeen carriages, most of them filled with the grand ladies of the court and the royal Princesses; all in lovely light costumes and bonnets to match. Following these were innumerable representatives of all the crowned heads of Europe; then, amid deafening cheers and wild waving of handkerchiefs, the band began to play "God Save the Queen," and slowly came the light cream-colored horses, covered with glistening trappings, and we saw "the sight" of the day.

In the large state carriage sat the Queen looking remarkably well in a becoming black and white bonnet and dress of the same combination, and carrying a white satin parasol. Opposite her sat Prince Christian and the Princess of Wales—the latter charming in an exquisite creation of pale violet. After these more soldiers, the beefeaters from the Tower in their queerly quaint costumes, the colonial procession, the Premiers and their wives, numerous troops on foot and mounted, and then—the most gorgeous, magnificent pageant we ever expect to witness, the great Diamond Jubilee procession, was ended. Ten minutes later the throng had dispersed and we had taken our train for St. John's Wood.

☾ *Prince Christian of Schleswig-Holstein (a large area in northern Germany) was the husband of Victoria's fifth child, Helena.*

The title of Prince of Wales was always bestowed upon the eldest son of the reigning monarch, in this case Albert Edward (Bertie), who became Edward VII when his mother died in 1901. His wife, Alexandra (see Page 53), was therefore the Princess of Wales at the time of the Jubilee in 1897.

E. Side, Poets Corner, Westminster Abbey.

Portland's Poet

$\mathbb{R}$ELUCTANTLY, WE REALIZE, the time has come when we too must say goodbye to our cheery little landlady, who from first to last has given us of her best, not only home and its belongings, but a cheerful, willing service such as money seldom buys.

We turn once more to old Westminster for one last parting glimpse. We seek again one hallowed spot, one shrine which draws unto itself the hearts of all his countrymen.

We stand before the likeness of a king, whose outward sign of royalty is seen but in the lofty brow, the throne of intellect, and in the strong and noble face which speaks in sculptured marble of a life of spotless purity and helpfulness. Far mightier than any earthly monarch is he whose realm embraces the entire world; whose verse, more powerful than any scepter, sways the hearts of countless men and women. We read again as we have often done with pride and reverent love the record of his birthplace—"Portland, Maine"—and feel upon us rush, the passing brightness of reflected glory in the deathless fame of our beloved—Longfellow.

"Bidding Farewell to the Metropolis"

HOW IS IT POSSIBLE in this last "London" letter to sum up all the delights and wonders of our stay? We have not written of "Sarasite," *(sic)* that wizard of the violin, who held us spell-bound by his matchless playing, now delicate and dainty as we imagine must be the tread of fairy feet; again full and resonant his tones, as though a hundred skilled fingers were concealed beneath his ten.

We have not even mentioned delightful talks and lessons with Mr. Virgil on our favorite practice Clavier. And did we not see and hear on her opening night in London, Bernhardt, the incomparable?

❦ *The September, 1894 diary of John Carroll Perkins (Minister at Portlands' First Parish Church) tells us more about Professor Virgil:*

"Mr. Kotzschmar, who has been our organist for over forty years, returned last Friday evening, (Aug. 31) from New York where he has been with his wife and others studying the clavier with Professor Virgil, the inventor. He returns enthusiastic over the method of this new instrument for piano practice. It seems destined to be very popular. He will teach this method."

90

Space fails us to tell of the beautiful statue of Siddons, unveiled by Sir Henry Irving, and of his most graceful characteristic speech; of operas, of Richter and Motel concerts; but we must describe the Commemoration concert on Sunday afternoon, June 20th. We sat with "beaming eye" and smile, delighted, before a note was sung, at the idea that we were to see Drs. Martin and Bridge, leading London musicians, and watch Randeggor conduct and see Cowen, whose charming music we love.

The Jubilee is over and ended is our stay in London. Days and weeks have slipped by, making two memorable months, overflowing with enjoyment. By twos and threes our party has separated, going several ways, and leaving the original "WE" in the little home in St. John's Wood.

☾ *Here are brief identifications of some of the names Mrs. Kotzschmar mentions in her writing:*

Pablo Sarasate (1844-1908) was an internationally known violinist, born in Columbia.

A. K. Virgil, an American, invented the Virgil Practise Clavier—actually a box with a piano keyboard without any sound-producing mechanism except something that produces a slight click if the key is struck properly. Mr. and Mrs. Virgil

SARASATE

also produced several books of exercises to accompany its use. The apparatus was popular both in England and America in the last years of the 19th century. Mr. and Mrs. Kotzschmar were excited about the Practise Clavier and even studied with Mr. Virgil in New York City in 1894.

Sara Siddons (1755-1831) was a famous English tragic actress. She reached the height of perfection in her art and was thought to be unsurpassed by any player of any age or nationality.

Sir Henry Irving (1838-1905) was the first English actor to be knighted. He had a long theatrical partnership with Ellen Terry. His ashes repose in Westminster Abbey.

Hans Richter (1843-1916) was a horn player who was known during his lifetime as the leading conductor of Wagner's works. Richter's popularity and influence in Great Britain were great. He conducted the Halle Orchestra in Manchester, England for fourteen years.

Sir Frederick Bridge (1844-1924) organist of Westminster Abbey for more than forty years, occupied many posts as teacher and conductor in London. Bridge was also a prolific composer.

C. H. Randegger (1832-1911) was an Italian composer, conductor and singing master. He settled in London in 1854 and had a very successful career there.

Sir Frederick H. Cowen (1852-1935) was a pianist, composer and conductor. He held permanent conducting posts and also conducted at many music festivals. His best works are thought to be for full orchestra.

THE ISLE OF WIGHT

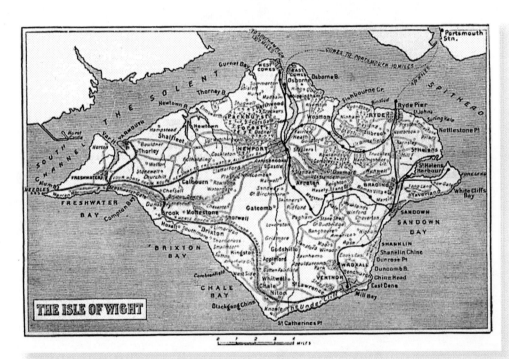

THE ISLE OF WIGHT

92

"The Isle of Wight: One of the Most Beautiful Spots in Great Britain"

"Omit seeing everything in England if need be, save the Isle of Wight," advised one enthusiastic friend. It is most satisfactory and delightful to follow advice, when it is exactly what one wants to do, as it certainly was in this instance. So we made an early start the Friday morning after the memorable Jubilee for the "British Bower."

It did not seem possible while in crowded London, that a ride of three hours by railway to Southampton would take us by banks and fields aflame with gorgeous scarlet poppies, past green meadows dotted thick with the gay blossoms, while still farther on we saw what looked like whole carpets of this same radiant hued flower. It was a sight we had often dreamed of, but the realization was so far beyond our dreams that it seemed as if, in this our first visit to the mother country, that Nature meant to show us that all our hopes and fancies concerning her could and would be fulfilled to the very utmost.

The delicious coolness of the sail across Southampton waters to Cowes, vividly recalled the invigorating breezes of Casco Bay, back home in Maine. We could not linger at Cowes, as we must push on to Newport for the night if we intended to be at Ryde for the grand naval review and illumination.

93

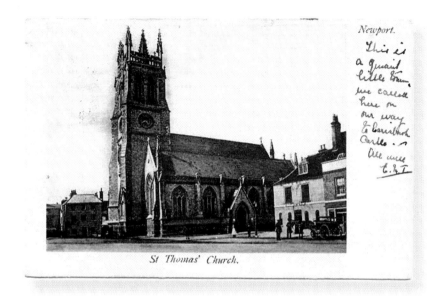

Newport.

This is
a quaint
little town
we called
here on
our way
to Carisbrooke
Castle…
All well
E. H. T.

St Thomas' Church.

NEWPORT

(O)UR NEWPORT INN, plain but comfortable, was close beside the parish church of St. Thomas. Our landlady gave us careful directions as to the locality of Carisbrooke Castle, the principal "show-place" of Newport. We hurried through the chambers of King Charles and the unhappy princess, anxious to give every moment of our time possible to the walk around the outer wall of the Castle.

There may be lovelier views of English meadows, divided by hedges of darker green and more graceful elms shading numberless little villages, with their ivy-covered churches, but we have not yet seen them. Whichever way we turned, a more charming picture than the last met our eye.

RYDE. — (Isle of Wight). — On the Pier. — LL.

"The Great Naval Review at Ryde"

R YDE DID NOT KNOW HERSELF Saturday afternoon; innumerable visitors thronged her charming Esplanade. The place itself was a "deserted village," every inhabitant being where a sight of the great naval review could be gained.

All eyes were turned toward the waters where England's mighty ships rode, and whither the nations of the earth had sent worthy representatives. The loud boom, boom of the cannon told us of the arrival of the Prince and we looked eagerly for the white flag of the royal yacht. We swallowed a huge lump in our throat as we saw a large "star-spangled banner" floating from the *Brooklyn*.

It was our first naval review and it certainly was a magnificent sight.

98

ESPLANADE.   RYDE I. O. W.

Our sail on the *Lorna Doone* took us around the fleet and gave us a fine sight of Japanese, Norwegian and other foreign visitors. When we crossed the line and saw before us those mighty battle ships extending for miles in one unbroken line, and we exclaimed "this is the sight of a life time."

How can we give even a faint idea of the beauty of the illuminations? Think of seven miles of electric lights, the masts and spars of each ship outlined with the dazzling globes, so close that it was one continuous line of fire. We stood at the end of the pier, and on both sides were ropes of red, white and blue lights, towers of blazing glory, and over all bringing them out in bold relief against the dark background of the sky, swept those powerful search-lights; it was a scene which beggared those produced by the genii of the lamp in the *Arabian Nights.*

100

VIEW FROM KEATS GREEN, SHANKLIN

LOVELY SHANKLIN AND ENVIRONS

THE OLD VILLAGE, SHANKLIN, I.W.

AT ELEVEN O'CLOCK that night—with many backward glances—we left for Shanklin. Our railway carriage was crowded three deep, the upper layer being entirely "Early English."

The remnant of a heavy shower which we had at Ryde, between the review and the illumination, followed us to Shanklin. In the morning our walks about the village, though not in the rain, were taken under dull skies.

Almost everything about Shanklin is in miniature, although it is growing rapidly. Tiny villas with roses climbing right up into the chimney pots, and such roses our eyes never beheld! They were in their glory, of every shade and all variations. Trees of yellow teas, great bushes of "Giant of Battles" covered with the regal rose "Baltimore Belles" running riot over plazas and in chamber windows—the roses alone repaid us for our trip!

BLACKGANG CHINE, VENTNOR.

WE SOON REACHED Shanklin's pride and glory, "The Chine." Surely there can be no lovelier ten minutes walk on earth. The steep sides of the gorge, rising high above us, were covered with trees; apparently every plant and trailing vine that grows hung in graceful lines form their roots and completely clothed what we knew must be rocks, but no color was visible but endless shades of emerald. Each leaf and blade of grass glistened from its bath the night before; we crossed rustic bridges, we heard a little brook go gurgling by, and at the head of the gorge we mounted higher till we overlooked the tops of tallest trees and saw a silver cascade dash down the steep rocky side; we cried once and again "how lovely! how exquisite!"

And then we kept silence for very shame, as we were so poor in words. Our guide left us with the warning to "keep the hill on our right," and leaving bay and sea on our left we prepared by tucking up our skirts for our four mile walk across the downs, through the landslip, by Bonchurch to Ventnor.

SHANKLIN CHINE

BONCHURCH, OLD CHURCH.

THE BEAUTY OF THE LANDSLIP is more wild than that of the "Chine" but in its way as attractive; one does not find here smooth paths and easy steps, but rather stony byways or wet and clay-like ground.

The woods were thick with wild flowers—yellow and white honeysuckles in masses peeped through thickets of ivy, snowy wild roses perfumed the air, but before we realized it we were declaring "Never was there any place as utterly charming as dear Bonchurch!" It is all of it within one's grasp as it were and we absolutely longed to put both arms around it and hold it close, it was so bewitching. The high cliffs from top to bottom were tapestried with ivy, relieved by great clumps of pink and red wild flowers; we wandered through the old church and saw the iron cross which—when the sun's rays fall upon it in a certain direction—cast upon the ground a perfect "shadow-cross."

Ventnor. St. Boniface from the Park.

106

VENTNOR FROM THE W.

WE CLIMBED UP, UP, UP the "chimney"—steep stone steps that took us on to the upper road to Ventnor, and gave us more charming views of land and sea. Ventnor is—Ventnor, what can we say more? Except each step was a new revelation to us of the beauty, the loveliness of Nature.

OUR DRIVE TO FRESHWATER AND ALUM BAY was delightful and the view of the "Needles"—chalk cliffs—most peculiar and interesting, as were also the pink, yellow and purple sands, of which we collected specimens. Yet, for us, the most glorious drive in the Isle of Wight was the "Undercliffs," from Ventnor to Blackgang Chine. A perfect road, thickly wooded on either side, whose trees meeting overhead formed oftentimes for nearly a mile, a leafy bower; the ivy and trailing vines seemed scarce able to find a place to cling, and each tree trunk was entirely hidden by the luxuriant growth of creeping things.

The tiny church at St. Lawrence, only large enough to seat fifty people, and which even a skeptic must enter with a bowed head (if he should exceed five feet in height) was one of the picturesque bits in the landscape.

All too soon we reached our goal, and began to descend "Blackgang Chine;" extremely black it was, all verdure gone, wild and rugged—no change of scenery could be greater; but we gained magnificent views of island, sea and lighthouse.

Steps make the descent—and it is a very, very, long one—extremely easy. We felt exhilarated from our drive and fairly danced down those winding stairs beaming with smiles. Suddenly we met a party of breathless, transpiring, Ascending (with a capital A) tourists. They almost glowered at us, as if our high spirits were a personal affront, and then gasped, with painful pauses between each word, "You—don't—know—what—you're—doing; it's—all—right—going—down—but"—here breath utterly failed.

This eloquent pause was amply filled twenty minutes later by two dejected disheveled females, who as they clung to the rope railing, breathless and almost sinking with exhaustion at each additional step, remembered their advance fellow sufferers whom now they repented themselves of secretly deriding, and fully realized that those same travelers had their revenge.

Merton College. Front Quadrangle, Oxford

UNIVERSITY"

❨ *July 5, 1897 found Mrs. Kotzschmar and her friends in Oxford, on their way to Scotland.*

It was "Commemoration Week" when the founding of the ancient university is celebrated. Two members of the group were fortunate enough to have a ticket that admitted them to the exercises in the Sheldonian Theatre. However, "WE" had but one ticket between them. Desperate to be in on the excitement, they came up with a brilliant plan. The two alternated entering—one went in to the first half, and the other took the seat after the intermission! This was a triumph, but more excitement followed.

Collections of Maine Historical Society

THE SURPRISES OF THE DAY were by no means over. Later, while on our way to Merton College, casually glancing down a side street, we thought we recognized a familiar figure. We looked again and in an instant were joyfully shaking hands with a prominent Portland minister, the Rev. Mr. Perkins. Mr. and Mrs. Perkins had landed at Liverpool only the previous day, and afterward we had the pleasure of calling on them at their hotel.

111

❨ *The Rev. John Carroll Perkins was minister of First Parish Church in Portland, Maine, from 1891-1913. Hermann Kotzschmar was organist and choir director at First Parish from 1851 until 1898. At the time of this trip the two were working together.*

EAST GATE, WARWICK.

WARWICK MILL STREET

St. Mary's Church, Warwick.

WARWICK AND SURROUNDINGS

I F ANY FOOTSORE AND WEARY TRAVELER, desiring a few days in which to recuperate, longs for the quiet of home where beds are downy and the table excellent, let such a one seek "Shakespeare's Inn" at Warwick; it is all there, what everyone has read about and wanted to experience. The pleasantest, most comfortable of landladies—Mrs. Hunt—the neatest and deftest of English maids, to attend to all material wants.

Warwick is the most convenient starting point for all excursions, and the drives are dreams of quiet beauty.

☾ *The group used lovely Warwick as a center for several daytrips to surrounding sites of interest.*

It needs a Walter Scott in the flesh to build again, to the sight-seer's perfect satisfaction, the ruined Castle of Kenilworth. Though the spot is indicated where the banquet-hall was, yet the thick carpet of green sward, the ceiling of blue heavens with only a fragment of ivy-mantled wall remaining, require a most vivid recollection of the great romance to recall Kenilworth's former glory.

Banqueting Hall, Kenilworth Castle

☾ *Kenilworth is a town in Warwickshire, popularized by Sir Walter Scott in his 1821 romance novel of the same name. The story is set in 1575 during the reign of Queen Elizabeth I, and takes place in Kenilworth Castle.*

114

WARWICK CASTLE

LORDLY WARWICK CASTLE'S MAGNIFICENT GROUNDS and luxurious interior give evidence of wealth and unremitting care.

We were specially interested in the noted French painting of the Countess which hung in the Castle, and we inquired of the condescending gentleman in gold lace and many medals if it was a good likeness. Instantly we found the question to be a fatal mistake. "Madam," was the answer in stern and surprised tones, there never was, there never could be, a good likeness of anyone as beautiful as the Countess of Warwick; it is simply impossible to represent with brush and paint such loveliness. This did not tally accurately with what we had previously heard outside the castle walls, but fearing imprisonment for doubt we blushed and deprecatingly moved on, by request.

The wonders of the art gallery were shown—the king-maker's historic mace—and a peep given into the dining-room resplendent in crimson and gold.

116

Stratford-on-Avon. Henley Street showing Shakespeare's House.

BIRTH ROOM.

SHAKESPEARES HOUSE.

"How Poor They are That Have No Patience"*

IT WANTED EXACTLY FIVE MINUTES OF SIX that same afternoon—after we had sat on the chimney settle where Shakespeare won Anne Hathaway and visited the memorial theatre and church, that the donkey with his best foot foremost, and Thomas the driver with his whip much frayed at the end, drew rein before the "bard of Avon's" birth place.

Kind reader imagine (we cannot depict) our dismay when the keeper of the door, with a gesture of command, said in a most exasperatingly cheerful voice, "closed for the night ladies." In vain we argued, with that sometimes insensate being called "man", that if he would give us the five minutes the law allowed, instead of consuming it in conversation, we could see all we wished, even if we lacked time for meditation, but he was obdurate.

Then W descended from her chariot with determination in her step and fire in her eye, and discovered the custodians of the house—two kind and reasonable women, who on hearing the case showed us everything, to the evident discomfiture of the disagreeable man. Now comes the strange incredible part of the story. With grateful hearts we offered each of those dear sisters—a shilling— and it was refused! This was our first experience of the kind since treading British soil. "Think of us kindly," they both said; "'tis all we ask," and indeed we always shall, for we owed them much.

* Othello, II:3

KESWICK AND DERWENTWATER

Thirlmere and Helvellyn

Buttermere House, between Buttermere and Keswick.

WENDING THEIR WAY

A GREAT DEAL OF THE FASCINATION OF TRAVEL consists in giving way to the day's fancy, making plans and changing them at will. We felt for one brief instant that three days would give us such a fleeting glimpse of lake and mountain in northern England, that it would be wiser far to wait until some future hoped for visit; but when our train reached Birmingham we cast wisdom to the winds and, saying "a half lake is better than no lake," we sped on through a more rugged phase of English country than we had yet seen.

Grasmere from Dunmail Raise.

This is the way we went from Ambleside to Keswick on the drive. M. H.

We climbed steep hills, and fairly held our breath for fear a word or sigh might weigh too heavily a passing cloud and give us rain, the thing we dreaded most as spoiling views; but fate was kind, and on our drive by coach to Keswick gave us clear sights of Skiddaw and Helvellyn.

Occasionally a shower for several minutes would send us denser clouds of mists rising from the valleys; then the sun would break out gloriously on Wordsworth's stony seat and tiny dove-cote. We saw them all—calm Rydal waters, Grassmere, and the quiet resting places of England's famous poets.

The charm of Keswick, overlooking Derwent waters, tempted us to stay.

❨ *But the group elected to keep moving on, so they continued north, taking the train from Carlisle.*

The English Lake District, an area where several major poets lived or visited, is only 30 miles by 25 miles. The "Lake Poets" is a term applied to William Wordsworth (1770-1850), Samuel Coleridge (1772-1834) and Robert Southey (1774-1843), who all lived in the area. Visitors included Percy Bysshe Shelly (1792-1822), Nathanial Hawthorne (1804-1864), and John Keats (1795-1821).

120

Robert Burns and Burns Cottage

"In Scotland"

❰ *The travelers arrived in Glasgow to torrents of rain!*

WE WERE NOT AT ALL ENTHUSIASTIC over "the second largest city of the kingdom," but there certainly was a good reason. We challenge any place to seem attractive when the fog alternates with rain, and where the street and sidewalks are thick with mud.

Far more did we enjoy the "Bonnie Doon," the "brig" over which Tam O'Shanter rode in frantic haste and terror. "This is the very bed where Robbie Burns was born" said the keeper of the little cottage, pointing to the side of the room, into the wall of which was built the rude frame. "Did those dishes all belong to Burns?" we asked, looking with awe at exactly fifty blue and white bowls of one pattern ranged against the wall, and supplemented on the shelf above by as many plates of one size and similar coloring. "No," was the honest answer, "I put them there meself to help fill up and sort of furnish like the room." Disappointed, we turned away, for we had hoped to buy a relic from the apparently inexhaustible supply.

❰ *In a poetic matter, Mrs. Kotzschmar describes the River Ayr:*

Ayr below, and air above, constantly recalled the greatest of Scotia's poets; each wild flower, each cloud of heaven, breathed of him who loved them and who made the world see in them a new beauty.

MOUNTAIN, MOOR AND LOCH.
"Where Natures heart beats strong amid the hills."

Arrochar Mountains from Inversnaid Hotel, Loch Lomond

WITH A DEEP SENSE OF ITS PECULIAR FITNESS TO THE OCCASION, we softly hummed "All we like sheep" as we met in the station on Tuesday morning at 8:30, ready to meet our "personally conducted" party to take the train to Edinburgh.

The greater part of our way was to be by boat and coach, the first essential for the enjoyment of both conveyances being sunshine. When on board the boat we found the wind swept down from Ben Venue, Ben Ledi and Ben Lomond with a will. It whistled through our coats and wraps and tried to drive us down below, but grasping hats and capes we stood our deck, to feast our eyes on land and water made familiar by the "Wizard of the North."

☾ *"All we like sheep" is a chorus from Handel's great oratorio* **Messiah.**

The term "Wizard of the North" was applied to the poet Sir Walter Scott (1771-1832) from 1815 until 1820, when he published, anonymously, five novels about Scotland.

"Magnificent Lake and Mountain Scenery"

Loch Lomond from Tarbet Pier

❨ *The journey continued as the group boarded a coach driven by a Scotsman.*

AT INVERSNAID WE CLIMBED THE LADDER to our seat on the coach beside the typical Scotch driver, which seat we had chosen that we might hold converse with him in his native tongue. In answer to our anxious query about the weather, made in purest Gaelic, he proved a true prophet by saying, "Ye're going to have a guid day for the Trossachs, and it's wan in tin that's fine."

The journey between Loch Lomond and Loch Katrine was by grand mountain roads, and down those steep sides leaped many glistening cascades. We waited for our little craft by the shores of lovely Katrine, picked bog and bell heather, and listened to the varied notes of the bewitching bag-piper. There the piper was in all the glory of plaid kilt and 'bunnit." W whispered to E, "a picture quick!"

At first it was impossible to get it, for as though the inspired strains could only be produced by locomotion, up and down the Scottish minstrel strode. Silver finally made him pause, and never did a woman seem more anxious for effect. "Is the bunit ye'll have on or off, Miss?" and with a look that shamed Apollo, there he stood, and—snap—we had him.

FAIR KATRINE, more sheltered than Loch Lomond, equaled our expectations. We were surrounded, hemmed in, by mountains. We sailed so near to Ellen's Isle that by stretching out our hands we almost touched the trees that shaded it. Once more, and now for the last time, we left the steamer and drove through the delightful Trossach district. Smooth roads ascending and descending, with round top after round top, high on either side, clothed with verdure or with heather thick with buds that soon would flower; romantic Lochs lay at our right or gave us fleeting glimpses through green trees.

124

PATH BY THE LOCH, LOCH KATRINE.

THE TROSSACHS.   THE PIER, LOCH KATRINE.

EDINBURGH: PRINCES STREET & ART GALLERY.

The Nave, Holyrood Chapel

EDINBURGH

"LADIES, PLEASE STAND HERE," was the polite command, as some hours later we stepped from the railway carriage into that most beautiful of cities—Edinburgh. "WE" asked each other, "Why is human nature so constituted that when told to stand 'here' one longs unutterably to stand 'there?' But we obeyed, and in a surprisingly short space of time our procession of twelve vehicles moved, as all processions do "through the principal streets of the city."

We were disappointed in ourselves, for we expected when we stood in Holyrood "a great wave of emotion to sweep over us," and it utterly failed. As the dusty bed of Queen Ann at Hampton Court left us calm and unmoved, so these of Charles I and Queen Mary of Scotland did not produce a single thrill.

While in the palace we wished there "wad some power the giftie gie us" to feel as confident of our knowledge of history as did "Miss Mixtup." We came upon her bewildering the guide by insisting that he should indicate which one of the many portraits of Mary the poet Burns preferred. "Of course you know, she said, addressing us nonchalantly, "that Burns was in love with Highland Mary Queen of Scots; it is such a pity they could not have been married!" and she gave a sympathetic sigh. "I don't know what I should have done on this trip," she continued, "if it hadn't been for those history lectures last winter."

Mentally pondering if many tourists were this afflicted, we continued our sightseeing.

HOLYROOD PALACE AND ABBEY.

Holyrood Palace, Edinburgh.

The Castle and Princes Street, Edinburgh

128

Of all the sights of Edinburgh, the one which we recall with greatest satisfaction is "The Castle." Standing as it has for ages on that lofty massive rock, looking down on broad Princess Street with its graceful monument to Scott, its building after building of stone and marble, what city can produce its like?

ABBEY FEVER

AS WE LEFT ABBOTSFORD,
the "sleeping beauty"—a member of our group so named because she 'napped' the entire way through the Trossachs, exclaimed —

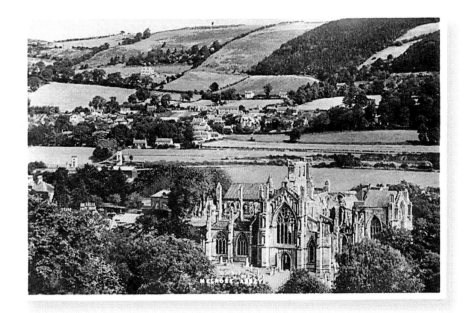

"Are you really going to Dryburgh Abbey? There's Melrose, and
one ruin is just the same as another!"

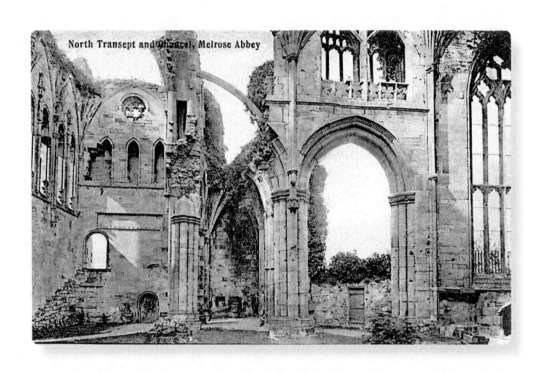

North Transept and Chancel, Melrose Abbey

WITH FEELINGS TOO DEEP FOR UTTERANCE, we merely answered "Yes."

"One ruin like another!" we repeated to ourselves indignantly; could we ever confound Melrose Abbey, with its exquisite carvings of curly kale and thistles, its symbolic window of the Crucifixion, with Dryburgh Abbey, where Scott is buried, wholly lacking the ornamentation of the first, yet surpassing it, we think, in charm of foliage and flower and fern.

133

The many appealing notices we saw about the Abbey grounds, beseeching visitors not to carve their names on the ancient tombs, were of course intended for other nationalities than ours. No American, we are morally certain, would ever be guilty of such an act of vandalism. We were equally positive we were not concerned with the following restriction—"Picnic parties absolutely forbidden in the graveyard!"

"About Cathedrals"

DURHAM CATHEDRAL

Seeing three Cathedrals in as many days made us most devoutly wish we had been reared on "Rehitecture" as well as "Reading, Riting and 'Rithmetic." For our lack of knowledge, however, concerning Norman, Early English and later Gothic styles, we could in some measure compensate by reverential admiration.

Certain travel-worn tourists have foretold that in a month no power on earth can induce us to look through even the doorways of the multiplicity of cathedrals that will fall to our appointed lot as sight-seers. All we can answer is now we are eager for more, and so far each one has, in our mind, its own distinct individuality.

THE CASTLE AND CATHEDRAL OF DURHAM, "half house of God, half castle 'gainst the Scot"—how high they stand on that bold rocky precipice, whose hoary side bearing all shades of green, with the river flowing at its base, together make a perfect instantaneous impression.

Inside the walls, the heavy pillars with their varied marking, the blending of the earlier and later styles so clearly manifest even to our sense, these cannot be forgotten.

York has its own peculiar charm; quiet as all cathedral towns, our Sunday there seemed like a benediction. We walked slowly to the Minster, our seats so near the lectern and pulpit that service and sermon were a new delight. It did indeed seem good for us to be there, and rested and refreshed in mind and body, we turned away, pausing beside the great stained window, through which the sun made quivering paths of light from side to side above our heads.

"This is my noblest work," the record reads of one, who, lying on his back suspended high in air, carved day by day the figure of the gentle Virgin, and as we gazed far up those tender eyes looked down, and seemed to say, "He labored long for love."

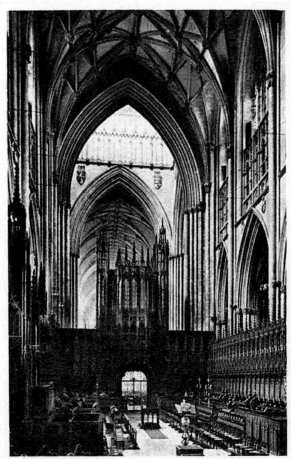

CHOIR LOOKING WEST, YORK MINSTER

LINCOLN CATHEDRAL

"**There! There it is!**" we cried with one accord, as we drew near to Lincoln. We had been looking eagerly from our railway carriage window for a sight of the cathedral, and before the city came into view we saw the hill crowned with its large carved tower, and bearing smaller ones on either side.

We walked about it later, lost in wonder, thinking of the years on years of patient toil that chiseled out of senseless stone those tiny leaves, those noble mullioned windows; and then we stood silent by ourselves to fix in mind the lofty arches, the sculpture forms that make "the Angel Choir."

Said to be the Earliest Church Carving in England.

Angel in Saxon Church, Bradford-on-Avon.

138

In many a hidden place, in many a secret corner of those old cathedrals, the choicest carvings lie. Those priests and laymen worked for love of Christ and labored not as unto man, but unto God.

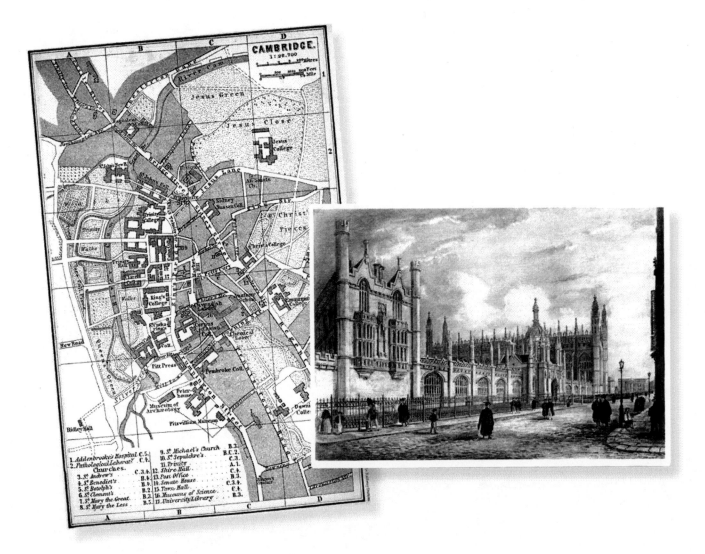

140

KING'S COLLEGE CHAPEL, CAMBRIDGE
THE ORGAN AND ROOD SCREEN

IVORY TOWERS

WE FOUND IT HARD TO LEAVE the "banks and braes" of Scotland, and even Cambridge, with its broad college walks shaded by many elms, its noted buildings—among them grand King's Chapel, could scarcely compensate us for making so hurried a visit to the North.

Minehead. View from Hopcott Lane.

142

"THE MOORS OF DEVON"

WITH **L**ONDON **AS OUR CENTRE** our travels have taken us to all four points of the compass, and we unhesitatingly declare that "West is best."

As little children often hoard their choicest morsel so we have saved our trip to Devon till the last. No "dove let loose in Eastern skies" o'er took homeward flight more swiftly than "WE" after reaching London. We left our party (who were to spend the next few days in seeing what we had already enjoyed), flew to Cooks Travel,

dropped our bills, folded our pinions, and took the train for Minehead—a six hour's continuous ride in the railway carriage.

☾ *"The dove let loose in eastern skies" came from the* **Oremus Hymnal: Companion to the Book of Common Prayer, 1890,** *used by churches in the Anglican tradition. Mrs. Kotzschmar was confirmed at Portland's St. Stephen's Episcopal Church in 1867, and was married there in 1872.*

BATH AND BRISTOL seemed most attractive but W was absorbed in contemplating a new variety of sheep of a lovely reddish brown hue, which here made their appearance for the first time.

Drawing E's attention to them she said, "That's worth remembering, Devon sheep are brown."

Out came the note-book and an item was written which afterward afforded E much amusement; when the driver of our coach, in giving us full information about the country and characteristics, incidentally remarked "How very brown sheep get lying by the roadside because there's so much iron in the soil." That's worth remembering," E began to quote mischievously, when an appealing maternal glance restrained her.

Porlock   Coach at Ship Inn.

REACHING MINEHEAD, not only did we climb the ladder, but stepped over intervening seats, until we reached the topmost pinnacle of the bright yellow coach. Loud and long rang the horn of the guard. Crack! Went the whip of the driver, and, beaming at each other, the passengers and the scenery, we were off for the hills, dales and great moors of Devon.

Those steep ascents where we rose ever higher and higher seemed like immense chess boards, each square divided from its neighbor by hawthorn or holly hedges. The many "combes" delighted us, deep clefts or gorges densely wooded and all crowded by the glorious moors, over which swept the freshest, most exhilarating air.

Lee Abbey & Bay Lynton.

LYNMOUTH FROM MARS HILL

Beautiful Lyn

WHEN WE HAD REACHED the highest moor and paused to give the panting horses a short rest, the descent began that brought us in the end to Lynmouth. The sun was shining bright on one side of Lynmouth Bay, while on the other towering cliffs with sweeping trees and creeping vines continued all the long way down; suddenly the charming villas and vine-clad houses came in sight, and we heard the swirling sound of East Lyn water.

Lynmouth nestles at the foot of Lynmouth Hill, the steepest climb of all, which fairly made us hold our breath, and there we reached our stopping place, Lynton. There would we gladly spend a summer and each day find some fresh charm. In no spot have we met more kindly welcome or seen more lovely country; hills and valleys, with the sea, making a combination as delightful as it is unusual.

147

LYNMOUTH AT WATERSMEET

THE SHADED WALK TO "WATERS MEET" is known to every visitor to Devon; here W, standing on a stone, marked the exact meeting place of Lyn and Badgeworthy waters, so that E's Kodak might faithfully picture all points of interest.

Morning Glories

THE NEXT MORNING at nine o'clock, our wagonette with horse and driver stood ready, and with everything we could wish for, sun included, we began our day's adventures. "Indeed ma'am I will show you everything," our young man said most earnestly, and he faithfully kept his word.

The path where John Ridd walked so many years ago to meet his Lorna, the very stones which formed the old foundation of the Doone hut, the church where John was wedded, all made the Devon story more real than we had thought was possible.

Three months even, have not accustomed us to the luxuriance of English vegetation. Each succeeding week brings its new and more beautiful wild flowers. We made the pony walk or stop to please our whim, gathering bunches of gorgeous purple foxgloves, and filling our hands with pale crimson birds-eye; the very stones were covered thick with dainty shades of rose and yellow stone-crop mixed with white.

All too soon we reached "The Lorna Doone"—a tiny farm.

EVENING DELIGHTS

WHEN WE RETURNED AT NIGHT, our hostess put before us such a feast as can be found only at Lynton.

We will not linger over chops and peas but pass the clotted cream and whortleberry tart, the very memory of which still brings the moisture to our lips.

☾ *Whortleberries are tiny blue-black berries, smaller even than Maine blueberries. Native to Devon, they are considered a traditional delicacy.*

Ilfracombe, Capstone Parade & Town

152

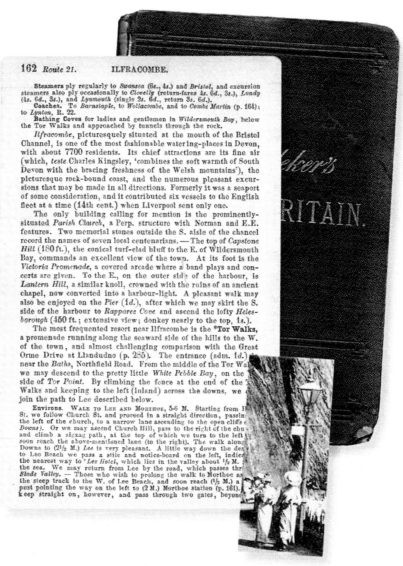

Ilfracombe,
in spite of its
melodious name,
proved something of
a disappointment,
so with no regret
we left the gay
watering place
behind us.

153

Clovelly from Hobby Drive

Clovelly Harbour

NEW INN

HIGH STREET, CLOVELLY.

WE HASTENED ON TO QUAINT CLOVELLY, so different in every way from any other spot in Britain. Our three mile walk through the "Hobby drive," amidst the wildest natural scenery, brought us in the end to an almost perpendicular cliff; here looking down we saw, built upon its steep sides, the one street which makes this most picturesque of places.

This street (there is no sidewalk) is paved with cobble-stones down which we plunged, until a rude stone step stayed threatened disaster. Succeeding this another plunge, and then a second step just in the nick of time, and so on till we reached the foot.

The houses touch, they are built so close together, and nearly each one had a small veranda embowered in vines, and all the tiny garden plots were filled with flowers.

There was a time, long past, when travelers sought here a resting place "far from the madding crowd," but frequent cheap excursions have changed all that. The day we spent there the place swarmed with picnic parties, tourists, and a sprinkling of visitors for a week.

The shining bay—the little harbor crowded thick with ships—the sailor "with his eyes grown blue" in the fronting of the sea—there they all were, and in each and all we found a fascination new and strange that clings to every part of fairest Devon.

☾ *Far from the Madding Crowd is the title of Thomas Hardy's fourth novel, one of a set titled* **Wessex Novels.** *Hardy took the title from line 74 of Gray's famous* **Elegy in a Country Churchyard,** *discussed on Page 62.*

FOLKESTONE HARBOUR, THE S.E.S.S. "DUCHESS OF YORK."

The dreaded channel crossing might have been experienced in a vessel much like this.

CHANNEL CROSSING

"**B**REATHES THERE A WOMAN with soul so dead, who never to herself hath said—'Paris! My dream, my longed for land!'" Even if in order to realize the dream, and reach that city of light, she must cross the ever-dreaded English Channel.

There are subjects to which the feeble powers of woman cannot do justice, and one is the passage between New Haven and Dieppe by night-boat. "The channel is all right" declared one man, "the trouble is with the boat."

Indeed, the water was scarcely stirred by a ripple it was so still, but the steamer, instead of carrying her allotted 140 passengers, was packed with 470! There were 51 plush-covered narrow boards, on which 150 first cabin females were to enjoy (?) a refreshing night's rest. We never prided ourselves on our mathematical dexterity, and we were surprised at the rapidity with which we subtracted 51 from 150 and found that exactly 99 remained. We were of the elect few who secured berths, the unfortunate 99 were stretched in corners, across chairs—sans air, sans sleep, sans everything; there was nothing for them to be thankful for but a calm sea.

At four a.m. we huddled together on deck for a breath of oxygen, a miserable looking group of objects, declaring that one such experience would last a lifetime.

❮ *"Breathes there a man with soul so dead...." is the first line of the Sixth Canto of* **The Lay of the Last Minstrel** *by Sir Walter Scott (1771-1832), one of the 19th century's most widely read writers. He established the form of the historical novel, and he was also a prolific poet. Many of his phrases are still in use today— for example, Mrs. Kotzschmar's quote (above), and "O what a tangled web we weave, when first we practise to deceive" from* **Marmion.**

158

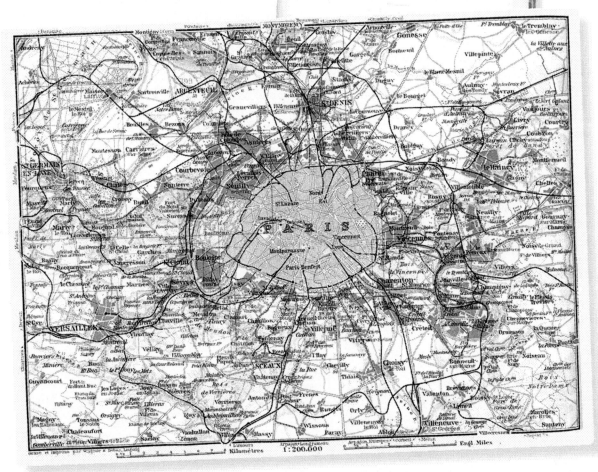

"IN PARIS"

THE COUNTRY BETWEEN DIEPPE AND PARIS may be charming—to our sleepy eyes it looked monotonous—the patchwork cultivation of the few gentle slopes, whose grains showed varying shades of brown and yellow was its most noticeable feature.

159

Soon the Eiffel Tower was outlined against the sky, then Paris!

"Paris at last!" we cried, and then hurried forth to meet the modern Circe.

☾ *Circe is the witch in Homer's* **Odyssey** *who captures and casts spells on Odysseus and his companions. Mrs. Kotzschmar must be referring to the many delights of Paris, which lure and detain visitors from all over the world.*

PARIS — Le Trocadéro

160

(O)UR FIRST DESIRE was to get a general view of the city from a height, and though that blot upon the landscape, the Eiffel Tower, was in our path, we passed it to reach "The Trocadero."

Not only is this building beautiful in itself, with its odd wings extended far on both sides, but from the top a noble panorama lies before one; not blurred and flattened as from the Eiffel Tower, but separate structures can be identified.

The towers of Notre Dame, the gilded dome of Napoleon's tomb, the Pantheon, all loomed up before us, and with at least a faint conception of the magnitude of the noted city, we began our tour of the churches.

162

- PARIS. - Boulevard Montmartre

"In and Around Paris"

❦ *Mrs. Kotzschmar gives her opinion about sightseeing on one's own, in contrast to the conducted tour:*

FOUR DAYS IN PARIS and not even a glimpse inside its fascinating shops is a record of which few women can boast; it may be well to explain that this self-denial was more compulsory than voluntary.

When tourists are "conducted," it is "go now" to this or that, or lose it. This, like most things in this world, has its advantages and disadvantages about equally divided. It is for the individual to decide if the comfort of having no care of tickets or hotels, no distress of mind concerning luggage, to leave the "lift" and find box and bundle already in one's room offsets having everything planned to a moment—no lingering in pet places and being eyed as a member of one of those abominations—a "personally conducted" party.

We number but few over twenty, and have more liberty than many; personal tastes are consulted in an unusual way, and gratified when in any way practicable. We can easily go where and when we please, provided we count the cost. That means additional expense, almost always loss of time, and often missing what we specially desired to see.

Sight seeing is a great art, and experience saves incalculable time and strength; so unless one is accustomed to travel, and has unlimited supplies of these two requisites, undoubtedly, at least for foreign-speaking countries, a conducted party is most simple, sure and satisfactory.

163

PARIS — Boulevard Poissonnière

164

AFTER WE HAD SEEN THE GREAT WONDERS OF PARIS, we were allowed to gratify our feminine thirst for shopping. We well know that many a woman's heart throbs with envy when she thinks of our opportunity to secure loves of bonnets, dreams of dresses, and the thousand and one airy trifles so dear to the female heart.

But let no one be under the delusion that beautiful things can be had in Paris for a song. Nay, nay, a good article brings a good price in Paris, as in New York; and just as charming creations can be bought in the latter place for the same money. We admit there is a halo surrounding the chapeau personally purchased in Paris which cannot be seen shining around the one bought at home, even if imported; but hats are difficult to carry in a trunk or in one's hand, and a woman with a bandbox has long ago gone out of fashion.

So with Spartan courage we bore the wolf-like gnawing of wanting everything, and said "it doesn't hurt a bit" when we withstood those tempting costumes. Truth to tell, we failed to see the advantage gained by one woman, who bought for herself and daughters twelve silk skirts at exactly the price asked in Portland, planning for each to wear four on their way through the custom house, and anxiously asking if they would be searched!

Museum Hopping

OUR VISIT TO THE LUXEMBOURG was most enjoyable, one great reason being that it is within one's power to gain some idea of its contents; though it would take days to see all the beauties of Detailles' great picture of the *Capitulation*. It hangs low, so that it can be seen two rooms away, and the effect of life is marvelous. One hears the measured tramp of men moving slowly along, with arms retained, for bravery, but with heads bowed low with grief.

More touching than scenes of war, more fascinating than Bonheur's beautiful cattle, was the picture that spoke of the utter abandonment to grief of one whom death had deprived of the sole treasure, and who, stricken, sought at the feet of the *Mother of Sorrows* sympathy and sustaining strength. All this we found in Bougereau's *Consoling Virgin*.

PARIS. — Le Jardin du Luxembourg.

PARIS. — Musée du Louvre, la Galerie des Rubens.

THE LUXEMBOURG IS POSSIBLE, THE LOUVRE IMPOSSIBLE—with its immense galleries filled with vast treasures of marble and painting—impossible to any but those with weeks of time at their command.

The miles on miles of Rubens and Van Dycks we could only glance at, but studied long Murillo's *Assumption* and the inscrutable face of Mona Lisa. Even the most enthusiastic love of pictures cannot prevent the eyes from tiring, or the head from aching with long looking.

☾ *Bartolome Esteban Murillo (1617-1682) was the first Spanish painter to achieve renown throughout Europe. His many religious paintings (**Assumption** was painted in 1670) depicted the peaceful, joyous aspects of spiritual life.*

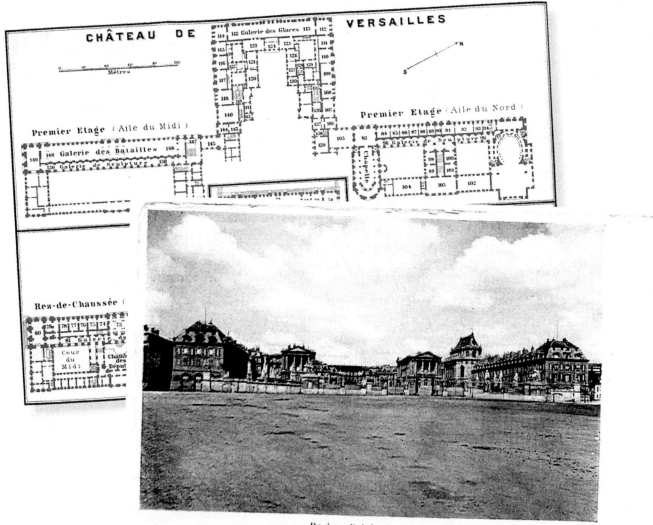

CHÂTEAU DE VERSAILLES

Mètres

Premier Etage (Aile du Midi)

115 Galerie des Glaces 115

Premier Etage (Aile du Nord)

Galerie des Batailles 148

Galerie de Sculpture

Chapelle

Galerie

Rez-de-Chaussée

Cour
du
Midi

Chambre
des
Dépu...

168

Importé.

Paris.—Palais de Versailles.

"Seeing the Beauties and Attractions of Versailles"

❦ *While at dinner one evening, word was passed among the members of the party that carriages would be ready to start for Versailles at nine the next morning. It was to be a day-long adventure!*

WE HAVE HEARD OVER AND OVER that it is "very foolish to try to see everything" but we know that not a woman lives who wouldn't rather look at the things she couldn't, than anything else on earth.

This disappointment somewhat clouded the day's brightness, and we felt somber when the graveled courtyard utterly barren—save for some startlingly white statues of some noted Frenchmen—and the seemingly low building, of vast area, of the Palace of Versailles were in front of us. But all thought of exterior vanished when we stood in those mighty halls, and walked through a few of those almost interminable rooms. Think of looking at eighteen miles of battle pictures! It was an impossibility even though they were by the greatest French painters of war scenes.

The apartments of Marie Antoinette were opened for us, and many of her personal belongings pointed out, but we have been shown such an unlimited number of writing desks and tables, used by that unhappy lady, that our credulity is exhausted if the supply is not.

WITH EYES BLINDED by the brilliancy of the "Galerie des glaces," vistas of mirrors on both sides apparently stretching for miles; with head swimming from gazing up at pictures, and down at marbles and bric-a-brac, we sank into an antique chair for a moment's rest, when, seemingly from a trap door at our feet, instantly appeared a gold-liveried three-cornered-hat official who politely assisted us to rise. Realizing that there is no "rest for the weary" in a palace, we sought the carriage.

THE GARDENS OF VERSAILLES, trim and artificial, yet imposing from their extent, the many fountains made us long to be there on some fete-day, when some sort of humanity fills every space, and music and all forms of entertainment combine to give a characteristic sight of French life.

OUR VISIT TO GREAT TRIANON, where Napoleon and later rulers retired for a space from cares of state, lost much of its attraction because we could not see the Little Trianon, which was undergoing certain repairs.

Versailles — Parc du Grand Trianon

❨ *Louis XIV had the Great Trianon built at Versailles in 1687, as a retreat far from the tumult of the court. Almost a century later Louis XV and Madame de Pompadour built the Little Trianon. It was given to Marie-Antoinette in 1774, and among other revisions she added an English garden.*

"The Gobelin Tapestries"

MANUFACTURE DES GOBELINS, Métier de Haute-Lisse

PERHAPS EVEN A GREATER GRATIFICATION of our curiosity was the forenoon spent in inspecting the Gobelin Tapestries; these are an exact reproduction, with needle, wools and silk, of paintings by the greatest artists. The workmen are years completing one piece of tapestry, so fine and laborious is the work upon it. Carpets of velvety softness were being made by hand, and everything manufactured belongs to the government, the articles being mainly used for presentation to foreign powers.

Sainte Chapelle...

WHILE ST. EUSTACHE is the most venerable church, the Madeleine impressive with its entire absence of windows, being lighted only from above, yet Sainte Chapelle is rightly named the jewel chapel, fairly blinded our eyes with its blaze of brilliant stained glass. The four sides are one mass of gorgeous colors; the robes of the marble saints and apostles studded with emeralds, rubies and diamonds. The red and gold of the ceilings, the inlaid floor all formed a striking contrast—as later we sat outside the open door, with the marble carvings of the exterior.

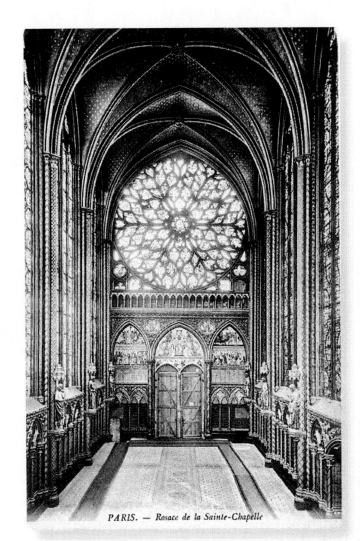

PARIS. — Rosace de la Sainte-Chapelle

PARIS. - Notre-Dame. - Façade. - Portail de gauche.
(Portail de la Vierge). - ND

...AND NOTRE DAME

THE "HOLY OF HOLIES" to the French people is "Notre Dame." What story, what romance, has been woven about its walls and towers. We looked at the ugly gargoyles, which Victor Hugo's hunchback thought were kin.

Slowly we walked down the nave followed by the sacristan who showed us the sacred relics brought from Jerusalem centuries ago by the good King St. Louis; golden vessels and precious stones of inestimable value, aside from their association.

PARIS. — Notre-Dame, Chimère. — ND

PARIS. — Notre-Dame. - Une Chimère.

PARIS. - Notre-Dame. - Chimères. - Chimaera. - ND

PARIS. — Notre-Dame. — Chimères

OUR WINDOW AT THE "GRAND TERMINUS" looked out on tableaux vivants so different from any we had ever seen, that we could scarcely leave it for needed rest. Small tables and chairs filled the sidewalks as far as we could see, up and down the street, leaving only a narrow passage for pedestrians. Here, from five in the afternoon until late at night, men and women congregate for dinner or to sip ices, and drink the many concoctions for which Paris is famous. Everything is orderly and everyone bright and intent on enjoyment.

Five of us contributed our share of amusement by sitting down one evening and ordering a "lemon squash" which is French for Yankee lemonade. The man of the party, while not an accomplished linguist, was an expert pantomimist. The dexterity with which he described to that garçon lemons, ice, sugar and soda-water, was inimitable. It convulsed the company at the neighboring tables; but the boy brought all, and manufactured before our eyes, the most satisfying, thirst-quenching beverage we had tasted since leaving home.

We walked to the Champs Elysses and the same gaiety was there only doubled and trebled.

How can one eat, drink and sleep, when the wonders of Paris by day and by night are within one's grasp? Paris by night! The stir, the excitement, must be seen and felt to be known.

180

"An Evening at the Paris Opera House"

UNQUESTIONABLY ALL TASTES CAN BE SATISFIED in Paris, from the meanest to the highest, and music is no exception to this universal; there is always variety sufficient for one and all.

We were delighted to find that Saint Saens' *Samson and Delilah* was to be given one evening while we were in the city, and a number of our party filled two boxes to see the world famous Grand Opera House, as well as hear a most delightful opera. Saint Saens' music reaches its most melodious height in the second act. Nothing could express love, more tenderly and passionately, than Delilah's great song, and the duet with Samson immediately following was equally charming.

The audience was composed almost entirely of tourists, so we could gain no idea of the brilliancy of a regular season night. The promenade about the magnificent foyer with its mirrors, broad stairways and statuary; it is impossible to adequately describe.

NAPOLEON BONAPARTE

THE NUMBER OF PUBLIC SQUARES AND PARKS in Paris is legion, and we saw them one and all with interest, as each has its historic association, but the glory of the Arc de Triomphe who can tell? Its wonderful proportions and ornamentation overpower one. It stands at the beginning of that long road of seven hundred continuous miles that ends at Milan with a similar arch—one of the mighty structures reared by Bonaparte for the admiration of coming ages.

PARIS
L'Arc de Triomphe.

PARIS — Le Tombeau de Napoléon 1er aux Invalides LIP   Tomb of Napoleon I

IT IS SELDOM THAT ANY OBJECT OF INTEREST made familiar by description equals one's expectation, but the Tomb of Napoleon surpassed all our preconceived ideas. Magnificent simplicity are the only words, contradictory as they seem, which can describe the impression made upon us.

The graceful marble pillars supporting the high altar—the sarcophagus, far below, cut from a single piece of porphyry—and encircling it on the floor beneath a laurel wreath, apparently painted in numberless tints of green and purple but which in reality is entirely inlaid with stones exquisitely shaded—all these produced an effect perfect and satisfying. The windows are so arranged that a radiant light surrounds the altar and tomb,

speaking day by day to the French people of the luster and glory that Napoleon once brought to France.

"No character of history is so difficult to estimate" said a voice speaking with authority, and what are we that we should weigh and measure, with our feeble capabilities, a man like Napoleon! He was mighty for good as well as for evil, and to call him a monster of selfishness is as far wrong as to hail him an angel of light. While he wrought much misery, the good he did exists today all over Europe.

"Yes," musingly the voice continued, "there has been in truth but one Napoleon; Vive l'Empereur!"

❮ *Porphyry is igneous rock containing large noticeable crystals, embedded in a much finer-grained ground mass. In smaller amounts it is an important material for paving and facing. In the ancient world it was quarried only in Egypt, and reserved for the use of the Pharaoh.*

On to Switzerland

IT WAS A WRENCH PAST COMPREHENSION, leaving Paris with so much unseen that we longed to see, and like the Scottish Queen we gazed at la belle France while its smallest portion remained in sight. We passed the woods of Fontainebleau, whose charms we could not fathom until another visit; we flew by many a little village and hamlet, and then gradually the country changed; plains gave way to hills, hills to mountains.

184

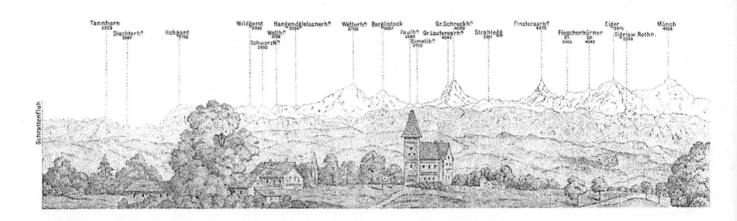

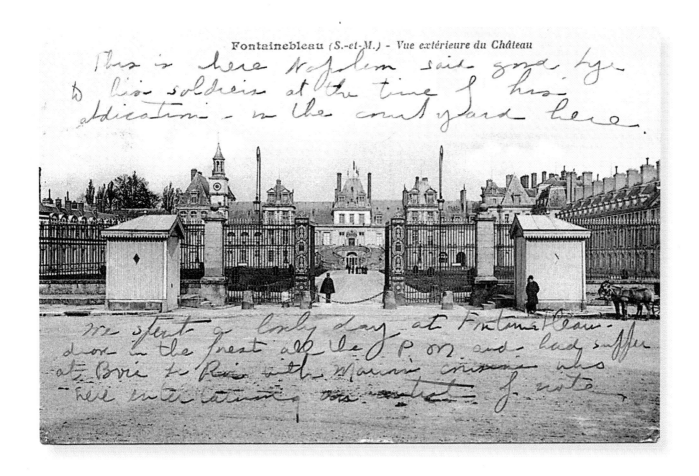

Fontainebleau (S.-et-M.) - Vue extérieure du Château

This is where Napoleon said good-bye to his soldiers at the time of his abdication — in the court yard here.

we spent a lovely day at Fontainebleau — drove in the forest all the P. M. and had supper at Bois le Roi with Maurice crimson who were entertaining ... of note

185

HIGHER AND HIGHER OUR TRAIN ASCENDED and glorious vistas stretched far on either side. Over mountain gorges we sped, gazing far down on valleys beneath, then without warning we would dart into a yawning tunnel, to emerge as suddenly on some view of lake, mountain and canton, still more beautiful.

A strong argument in favor of the belief of the Christian Scientist, that "as is the mind so is the body," may be found in the twelve hours' ride from Paris to Berne. The same amount of heat, smoke and cinders, on any less interesting route, would have been simply unendurable, but as we were on our way to Switzerland, and every mile brought to us new and more wonderful pictures, we did not notice blackened hands and faces, or realize weary frames.

Neuchâtel - Quartier de l'Ouest

188

Brünigbahn und Lu[...]

OUR RAILWAY CARRIAGE had a narrow passage with windows close together, and from two o'clock till eight, we were springing almost incessantly from side to side, fearful that the least bit of the unequalled panorama might escape us. Through narrow openings we caught sight of water, then all was darkness for a moment, to reveal later Lake Neuchatel, and, bordering it, miles of vineyards, with the streets and houses of Neuchatel.

A short distance farther on Berne was reached, and our journey ended for the day.

AN ALPINE TOWN

THE FOLLOWING MORNING we saw the city in holiday attire, from every window fluttered a flag, and banners of red and blue, black, white and yellow, were stretched across the streets; fountains were decorated with flowers, the streets filled with women, their black velvet peasant waists trimmed with large silver filigree buttons, and long chains of silver festooned under the arms from front to back, making them the envy of their visitors.

All this brightness meant that the annual Schutzenfest or shooting match, which is held at each canton in turn, was, this year, to be celebrated in Berne.

BERNER TRACHT - COSTUME BERNOIS.

192

Wengen.

Hôtel Victoria und Jungfrau.

Gruss aus Thun!

Lakes and Mountains

No tourist, we believe, who visits Switzerland fails to take the steamer trip on Lake Thun to Interlaken. Our afternoon was unusual, so an English woman told us who was sojourning among the Alps. "It is, in fact," she said, "the first bright, cloudless day for weeks," and such a vision as we had of the snow capped Jungfrau, was compensation for crossing the Atlantic.

The turquoise blue of lake and sky, the wooded mountains, with those fascinating Swiss chalets perched upon their sides, and towering above all those peaks covered with never-melting snow, could anything on this earth be more beautiful, grand and awe-inspiring?

194

Jungfrau 4166 m und Kl. Scheidegg

Interlaken — Höhenweg, Grands Hôtels Victoria und Jungfrau

INTERLAKEN, the busiest, gayest of little places tucked in among those mighty mountains— the shops, enticing with their articles the last centime from our pocket books—we found it all as we had dreamed for years it would be. We had lakes, valleys and mountains to our heart's content, and literally with our menu, for at table d'hote first one guest left the table and then another till all stood entranced before the Jungfrau Queen whose brow was glowing with "a light that never was on sea or land" but which sometimes falls to mortals to behold among those Alpine heights.

The setting sun, as he sank from sight, threw back a rosy radiance that colored snowy peak with light celestial, and left us feeling we had almost seen into the heaven of heavens and caught a glimpse of glory ineffable.

Our only disappointment throughout our trip has been that we could not see everything, and our great difficulty was to make choices among the many tempting excursions offered.

☾ *"A light that never was on sea or land" is Line 15 of William Wordsworth's poem* **Elegiac Stanzas.** *The inspiration for the poem was Sir George Beaumont's painting* **Peele Castle in a Storm.**

"Making the Ascent of the Mettenberg"

Glacier des Bossons

Our Sunday was spent in a state of indecision, as to whether we would on the following day take the absolutely perpendicular railway to the Schynegge Pass "and gain the view of our life" or climb the Mettenberg, with a small party led by the Professor. We retired leaving the burden of decision on the weather's shoulders. The day dawned somewhat dull, but promised fair, and we decided on the climb.

"Hark! Here's an avalanche" was said simultaneously as a thunderous sound echoed and reached across the mountains, followed by another and yet another. Then down fell ice and snow piling in fleecy masses before our eyes, and over and over on that memorable day did we hear that tremendous boom.

The danger of walking over those glassy frozen fields that had scarcely melted since the foundation of the world was now clearly manifest. Huge crevasses gaped on both sides, 900 feet in depth going down, down, farther than the eye could see and revealing mighty walls of indescribable blue. We planted our Alpen-stocks firmly in the ice, and swung ourselves across chasms where one slip meant—Eternity. We stood on narrow ice-paths looking into yawning gulfs, then gazing up, up, up to the eternal snows; feeling then and not till then, that we had some comprehension of the Alps, and of their silent awful loneliness.

Surely "on the heights" the littleness of our life-plane is most keenly felt, and every yearning after good becomes intensified.

W was in advance when a startled scream made her run back, fearing some catastrophe, although the cry seemed one of pleasant surprise; motionless stood a member of the party with a most beatific expression of countenance, while both hands adoringly clasped a small white, star-shaped fuzzy object, filled in the centre with pale golden French-knots.

W sank down in utter collapse, instantly realizing that she had not two moments before missed the opportunity of her life, and left to be gathered by another the only reward an Alpine climber craves—"Edelweiss." "There! There! Way up there are two more," the excited young woman screamed, pointing to a rock on which could faintly be discerned two pale gray leaves with a many-cleft snowy flower in the middle.

With Alpenstocks wreathed with flowers, triumphantly bearing the Edelweiss badge, the insignia of an Alpine climber, we marched to Grindelwald, and then back by carriage to Interlaken, which we reached at ten that evening.

198

Gruss aus Grindelwald.

Grindelwald · Kirche und Viescherhörner

"THE LION OF LUCERNE"

A succession of sunny days made us accept most unwillingly a rainy afternoon at Lucerne, but after Grindelwald and the Mettenberg, Interlaken and the Jungfrau, Lucerne's attractions were diminished, save for its immortal Lion, which far exceeded, in noble proportions, our expectation.

Our view of the Rigi and Lake Lucerne were exceptionally fine the day we left, as the rain had passed and light clouds added new effects. If we have made apparent the dexterity we exhibited in rushing from one carriage window to another on entering Switzerland, how is it possible to portray the lightning speed with which we chased these glorious views over the Brunig Pass, and later St. Gotherd, when leaving that country of mountains, lakes and torrents.

We utterly lack the power to describe the foaming cataracts that cast themselves in such utter abandon from the rocks, and sent their spray and mist high in the air; yet we were not satisfied with viewing each side alternately, and finally took up our position on the platform where we stood breathless as we passed under gigantic rocks which we could almost touch, and seething, angry torrents.

"The Charms of Italy"

WHILE EVERY LAND POSSESSES its distinctive characteristics that attract the traveler with the charm of novelty, there is a subtle something surrounding Italy, and Italy alone.

It is not only its blue unclouded skies and picturesque places, for under the former there is, in summer, scorching heat and in the latter innumerable discomforts, but the feeling awakened, the imagination kindled there can be experienced in greater degree we know only in far off Palestine.

202

MILANO   Galleria Vittorio Emanuele

MILAN

WHO CAN REALIZE PHYSICAL ANNOYANCES while listening for the call "Milano!" This was to be the "open sesame" that should spread before our eager eyes the treasures of Italia. A dreamless night's rest prepared us on the following day for "fresh churches and pastures new."

These we found without difficulty in the city which boasts the third largest cathedral of the world, and the galleries of Victor Emanuel. This latter, with its immense glass covered dome, is the favorite shopping place and promenade of the Milanese.

Milano - Piazza del Duomo - Mon. a Vittorio Emanuele II.º

Milano
Il Duomo

204

This gives but a faint idea of the great beauty of the carved stone which it 2000 figures — We see it for the second time and go up on the roof — July 20 N.C.C.

"The Milan Cathedral"

We did not realize in what direction we were moving, as we walked under the late king's triumphal arch, when lo! Fronting us was the mighty House of God. The surprise was so complete, the structure so stupendous, that we could only stand in awed silence before it.

Thousands of threadlike spires, each bearing a sculptured saint, rose high in the air; flying buttresses carved in many fantastic shapes, the most wonderful being the garden where every flower and fruit, wrought in stone, flourished in never-fading beauty.

206

FLORENCE

WITH ITS BACKGROUND OF RUGGED PYRENEES, its vineyards—where row on row of fruit trees were looped with vines loaded with purple and white grapes— its millions of olive trees and many wayside shrines—how beautiful the road that leads to Florence!

We fully realize that we only made our obeisance to that wondrous city, and that to know her as she was and is requires years of closest intimacy, and yet, with all we left unseen, we'd travel thrice as many miles to gain once more a fleeting vision of fair Florence.

☾ *Mrs. Kotzschmar could not have seen the Pyrenees on her way to Florence; what she actually saw were the Apennines, a mountain range in central Italy. The Pyrenees form a natural border between France and Spain.*

Florence, the home of Dante—of Michael Angelo whose *Day and Night, Morning and Evening* were a revelation in sculpture. Florence! Where Fra Angelico consummated in color the semblance of his heavenly visitants, and Giotto and Della Robia wrought imperishable monuments—we were as these stricken dumb, for speech "in wonder died away."

The treasures of the Uffizi and the Pitti Palace are overwhelming. We sat in the Tribune before the masterpieces of the world in painting and sculpture, and the magnitude of it all, we could not even faintly comprehend.

210

L'Anfiteatro Flavio o Colosseo con l'Arco di Costantino e la " meta Sudans „

"Rome: Pleasant Days Spent in the Eternal City"

W E ARE STRONGLY TEMPTED to send home a blank sheet of paper with one word in the centre—Rome! Knowing that one word will have a deeper meaning, and be more eloquent, than many sentences. "We are in Rome!" We've said it morning, noon and night, and looked into each other's faces for a transformation which we felt must have been wrought by an event which meant so much to us.

Thus far all things have been most propitious, none more so than the weather, and where we most expected extreme heat—in Italy—we've walked and driven at pleasure, and with less discomfort than we have often felt at home.

Despite all warnings we have drunk the water freely, and visited the Coliseum by moonlight; experienced travelers we met in Rome assuring us that now nowhere is water purer than in the large Italian cities, and that with improved drainage Roman fever has been practically stamped out.

❡ *In the paragraph above Mrs. Kotzschmar is referring to two health issues that concerned all international travelers. Intestinal diseases such as typhus and cholera were brought on by drinking contaminated water and "Roman fever" (as the English termed malaria), which was contracted by mosquito bites. Mosquitoes are more active at night, but their numbers were greatly reduced by the drainage of the swamps around Rome.*

211

212

Roma – Basilica di S. Pietro in Vaticano
L'Interno generale della Chiesa (XVI Secolo)

THE MAGNITUDE AND GRANDEUR OF CHURCH AND CATHEDRAL culminates in St. Peter's, so vast that the human mind fails to grasp its enormous but perfect proportions. The chiseled figures of Canova, the wealth of mosaics, gold, silver and precious stones; all the unequalled splendor of St. Peter's, made us feel that the half had not been told in book or picture.

While looking at the massive statue of St. Peter, a man came forward leading a little child whom he raised to kiss the shining toe of the apostle, then pressed his own lips devoutly to the spot; following him was an aged woman, then young girls, while priests upon their knees close by recited many orisons.

We sent the rosaries we purchased for the Pope's blessing but fear that hardly constituted us good Catholics.

❆ *Canova (1757-1822) was an Italian neo-classical sculptor whose work can be seen at leading galleries in Italy, as well as major museums in Paris and London.*

ROMA.   Il Colosseo (Interno).

214

Roma. Colosseo dal Palatino.

On a second visit to the Forum and Coliseum, Galio, the prince of guides, made all things live anew to three enthusiastic lovers of Roman antiquities. The triumphal Arch of Severus—the memorial carvings on Titus' Arch—to look on them brought back the former glory of the "mistress of the world."

We walked along the Via Sacra and each saw for herself the triumphs of Scipio and great Pompey. We heard the voice of Antony in burning words as when he spoke above the body of dead Caesar.

But beyond all other ruins, mighty and majestic, stands the Coliseum! Who so indifferent as to behold it without a moistened eye and quicker beating of the heart! Those walls have seen the centuries come and go and still they stand—the hand of time lies heavy on them, yet even in rain they mean—Rome!

❰ *The Via Sacra, or Sacred Road, which connected some of the most important religious sites in the Roman Forum, stretched from the top of the Capitoline Hill (one of the seven hills of Rome) to the area of the Coliseum.*

Scipio (236-184 B.C.) was the Roman general who invaded Africa, causing Hannibal to leave Italy and return to Africa to fight him. In 202 B.C. Hannibal was defeated by Scipio at Zama. Carthage surrendered her war fleet and Scipio returned to Rome a hero.

Pompey (106-48 B.C.) was a great Roman general who was victorious in many battles. He was defeated in a civil war with Julius Caesar.

THE RUINS OF POMPEII

WE AWOKE ONE MORNING to find ourselves confronted by the question—For the sake of visiting Pompeii, will you travel from 8 a.m. to 6 p.m. save for the three hours in which to walk through that long buried city? What power the early morning hours possess to damp ardor and quench enthusiasm! We had always supposed we longed for Pompeii with an unquenchable longing; but when the visit meant loss of morning nap, Pompeii was to us—as to its unfortunate inhabitants, but dust and ashes.

Panorama della Città con la strada dell' Abbondanza   Pompei

"We'll bitterly regret it if we don't go," was the spirit with which we urged each other on, and in a few hours the smoking mountain came in view, and the lava strewn country told us where we were. How real it made the city seem; to walk those narrow streets and see the rut-worn stones where chariots passed before the birth of Christ.

"The new house," unearthed not more than eighteen months ago, surpassed all in preservation and attractiveness. The Atrium with the very fountains and figures standing as the owner placed them, looked as it did two thousand years ago. The brilliant red of the walls, the still fresh frescoes, made it difficult to realize that they had been sealed from sun and air for centuries.

Vesuvius was on best behavior, though occasional sullen puffs of smoke told us of smoldering wrath.

Our plans were made for the ascent, but when we found that meant to forego Capri and Sorrento, the latter places conquered.

217

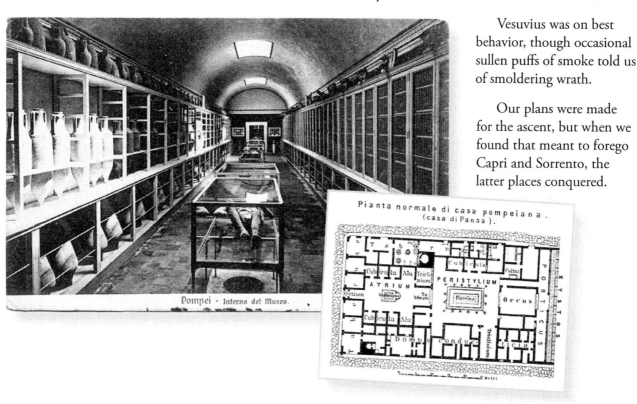

Pompei - Interno del Museo.

Pianta normale di casa pompeiana.
(casa di Pansa).

Naples: From Shore to Sea

WE HAVE HAD MANY RED LETTER DAYS throughout our trip, but that day when we sailed upon the Bay of Naples was a heavenly one, not only for enjoyment but as making known to us the meaning of "celestial hue." The blue depths of sky were mirrored in the same bright color of the water that gleamed about our ship.

NAPLES from the Parco Grifeo.

Upon one side of us rose Vesuvius, with many sister peaks, then Naples to which our distance lent not only enchantment but a much needed and appreciated sweetness—while music from guitar and mandolin with singing voices added the one charm desired.

Napoli L' eruzione del Vesuvio

Sorrento · Marina.

AH, SORRENTO

Now that we are ourselves in Italy, Claude Meinotte's famous flowery sentences and impassioned words seem natural speech, and we are tempted to say in feeble imitation, "Wouldst know the charm of orange bower, of oleander bloom, of scent, of Jessamine and tuberose? Wouldst feel in all its cooling freshness the balmy breeze that lightly blows from Naples Bay? Then linger at Sorrento; so strange its narrow streets, its rocky fortress walls, so bright its many shops with silken stuffs, and olive wood inlaid and carved in countless ways for use and beauty."

So dreamy, so alluring is Sorrento, we could not bear to leave; for the first time in our lives we revelled in an orange grove, we picked and ate the luscious fruit till we were satiated, and then with branches laden with the golden balls, we turned our faces back toward Naples.

221

For almost the first time, we pleaded guilty to being tired, and felt for the moment that nothing could interest us, but the sights of Naples would animate a graven image. The hour was six at night, and our drive took us along the principal thoroughfare of the city and by beautiful buildings.

❆ *Claude Melnotte was a gardener's son in Edward Bulwer-Lytton's 1838 play **The Lady of Lyons**. He was given to profuse and poetic utterances.*

"The Contrast of Plenty and Poverty"

The characteristic of Naples is its sharp contrast of wealth and poverty—of misery and happiness. Boys with tattered apologies for garments which scarcely held together were driving a herd of goats before them, stopping at various houses while the maid, with glass in hand, herself secured the evening's supply of milk, having an advantage in knowing that she had it fresh from nature's fount, without being diluted at the iron fountain.

NAPOLI - Porta Capuana

A haggard woman lay upon the pavement, and covering her were five sleeping children. A boy of six stepped from a tub of water placed on the sidewalk, while a curly-headed cherub of three stood ready to occupy the vacant bath.

NAPOLI - Piazza della Stazione

NOT ONLY WAS IT GOOD-BYE PIETRO, but good-bye to Italy for us. We realize now; even more than when we began our letter, that the power has not been vouchsafed us to make known the potent influence, the magic glamour, that surrounds that land of history and of art, and our first impulse to say nothing was the wiser one, for it is with feeling as with waters, "the shallows murmur, but the deeps are dumb."

☽ *"the shallows murmur..." was written by Sir Walter Raleigh (1552?-1618), a warrior and a scholar, who at one time attended Oxford. This quotation is taken from the beginning of his poem* **The Silent Lover.** *The poem opens with the lines "Passions are likened best to floods and streams: the shallows murmur, but the deeps are dumb."*

GERMANY

München, Hofbräuhaus

WE HAVE COMPLETELY LOST OUR HEARTS to
Germany and Munich was the first city
to win them; her broad, clean, tree-shaded streets, her
substantial buildings, her kindly people made us feel
at home the moment we stepped from the railway
carriage, tired and dusty from our two days and nights
of traveling.

München   Steinsdorfstrasse.

NUREMBURG

WE BETOOK OURSELVES to Nuremburg. We could fill pages with
descriptions of the quaintness of its long, narrow streets, its
many gabled roofs and small windowed houses, leaning toward each
other for support as if weary with the weight of years.

Nuremberg.

We stood long about the market place, a large open square with curious fountains, where the women bring their fruits and vegetables for sale, who in their peculiar costume and odd head-gear gave us many queer pictures.

We roamed about the castle and saw the execution-chair where but fifty years ago a prisoner sat, bound hand and foot while the swordsman with one swift stroke cut off his head.

Among countless instruments of torture we saw one peculiar to this ancient place—"the iron maid." She stood apparently smiling a welcome to the helpless victim; slowly the arms stretched forth, the form unhinged, the wretched prisoner was placed within the hollow, the relentless shape enclosed him, crushing out life while thrusting into his body hundreds of iron spikes.

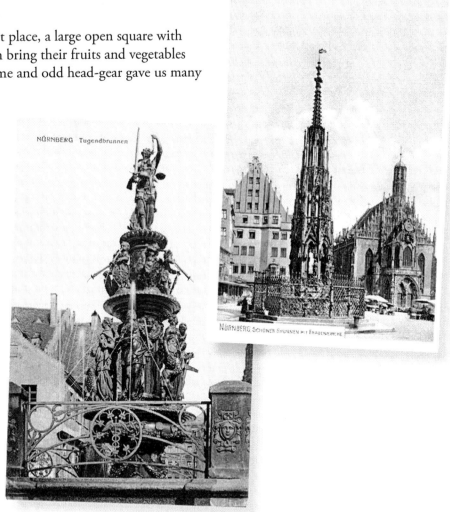

Grüning

Theater,
Vorder Ansicht.

Theater
Innere Ansicht.

Gruss aus BAYREUTH.

Richard Wagner

"AT THE SHRINE OF WAGNER"

NOTHING COULD HAVE BEGUILED US from fascinating Nuremberg but the power of the "Nibelungen Ring," that attracted us with irresistible force to Bayreuth, the Mecca which draws unto itself from the entire world the worshippers of Wagner's wondrous genius. Bayreuth was as the slumbering princess until the Master's magic music awakened her to life.

We reached our stopping place on Hofgarten Strasse, the day before the first performance of the last Cycle. What shall we do we queried, if they can't speak English? Our fears were only too well founded. Frau Methuselah the maid met us before the iron gate with cheerful German greeting, followed by the "Mistress of the Haus," with similar voluble welcome but by incessant turning of the leaves of our small dictionary we carried on a satisfactory conversation and were soon friends with all the household, including Hund the dog and Baedilah the cat.

We quickly discovered that we were but a few steps from villa Wahnfried in whose grounds Wagner lies buried, and soon we were standing before the ivy covered mound on the top of which rests a plain marble slab completely covered with fresh laurel wreaths and flowers. A feathery grove of young trees grow thick about the grave, and through them the sunlight filtered, casting faint shadows, while birds sang softly in their leafy branches of the final consummation of "Hope's Peace."

"Though dead he yet speaketh" we murmured involuntarily as with a vast multitude of all kindreds and nations, we walked slowly along Bahnhof Strasse through the double row of noble trees that line the way to the very entrance of Wagner's theatre, where the lofty creations of Wagner's genius are enacted.

While nothing could be plainer, outwardly, than the building, its situation is typical of the far-reaching power of Art. Standing as it does upon a commanding height, it sends forth through the wonderful interpretations that there take place, a glorious light that illumines musically the nations of the world.

229

❦ *"Though dead he yet speaketh" is a line from* The White Pilgrim, *written by John Ellis upon visiting the grave of his friend Joseph Thomas in 1838. The text was put to music in the Sacred Harp literature, so Mrs. Kotzschmar may well have heard it sung, as well as having read it.*

230

Emma Eames Story

A BEAUTIFUL STORY

IT WAS WHILE WAITING FOR THE OPENING SCENE of *Parsifal* that we first saw her, the loveliest woman among a thousand, whose dainty costume of light gray silk and the nodding black tips in the becoming hat, said plainly as words "we are from Paris." She was surrounded by a laughing group of friends, and as we slowly sauntered by, she exclaimed "I never was in better health in my life,"—then the trumpets sounded and we hurried to our seats, but W grasped E's arm and whispered "I know who it is, and I shall speak to her."

During the second pause all things were propitious; while looking eagerly around, we saw her standing with her husband, quite apart and in a moment we had spoken our name and were greeted with a most cordial hand-pressure. We talked of London and the successes she met with there and, naturally, of Bayreuth. "Yes," said the fair songstress in answer to our query, "Madam Wagner invited us specially for *Parsifal* and more than all wants me to sing at the next festival in '99 the role of Seglinda and Eva; I feel highly complimented, and shall remain abroad next year to study the part with Madam Wagner herself, for I wish, of course, in my interpretation to approach as nearly as I can the idea of the Master."

"Then," we said, "regretfully you will not sing in Portland's new opera house* for some time." "Has Portland a new opera house?" was the surprised rejoinder, "How delightful!" I shall look forward to singing there when I return to America."

And with kind messages to mutual acquaintances one of the pleasantest moments at Bayreuth was ended.

"How charming she is!" exclaimed E. "What grace," echoed W as we reached our seats, and congratulated ourselves on meeting one of the world's famous singers. It is seldom one sees a face that shows at once such strength and such sweetness combined. Maine has much of which she can boast, her rugged coasts, her island-dotted bay, her air and her people but she owns no fairer daughter, she claims no sweeter singer than **Emma Eames Story.**

231

❪ *Emma Eames (1865-1952), a lyric soprano, was born in Shanghai, China, where her father was a lawyer. She was brought to the United States when five years old and spent her girlhood in the home of her grandparents in Bath, Maine. After studying in Boston, she went to Paris and studied with Marchesi. She sang in the leading opera houses of America and Europe.*

*Mrs. Kotzschmar was probably speaking (modestly) of Portland's newest concert venue, Kotzschmar Hall, named for the city's premiere musician. Situated on Congress Street next to the Baxter Library, the intimate hall (about 500 seats) was described as "An Opera House Equal to Anything of its Size in New England." Its concert dedication was held November 10, 1891. In recent times the building fell into disrepair and was demolished in 2004.

232

Inneres der Kirche
Gruss aus Finsterwalde

❦ *Mrs. Kotzschmar speaks here of visiting the rural village of Finsterwalde, where her husband, Hermann Kotzschmar, was born in 1829. Mr. Kotzschmar emigrated to America in 1848, reached Portland, Maine in 1849, and never returned to his homeland.*

The postcard (left) and photo (above) show the 1549 Lutheran church in Finsterwalde, where Hermann Kotzschmar (at left, in a 1896 studio portrait) was baptized in 1829.

RELATIVE CONVERSATION

I REALIZE FULLY THE IMPROPRIETY of beginning with the first person singular, but 'tis done with deliberate premeditation, and in the outset let me state that this letter will, intentionally, bristle with "I's" being confident that when my reason is known I shall have the deep sympathy of all womankind.

For more than forty-eight hours, not once have I spoken to a fellow-being, so as to be comprehended. I've soliloquized, 'til Selkirk's attempts seemed as nothing; but now, individually, and in the first person, I must talk to the *Daily Press*. It is all a mistake to suppose that A. Selkirk's position was hard, because one expects only soliloquy on a desert island.

But the situation that is misery is to be surrounded by nephews, nieces and cousins, and all their friends and, though not deprived of the power of speech, yet to be unable to utter an intelligible word—that is a time which makes an uninhabited spot the most desirable place in the world.

To change slightly the old Sunday School hymn—"I have a brother in the German land, my brother called me, and I went to meet him, in the German land," thrusting aside and ignoring the consciousness that I could not speak his language, and he knew not one word of English. "There are the children, of course they study it in school," I said, laying my burden on their young shoulders, forgetting F. was a small old-fashioned German village, miles from the direct line of communication with the great cities, and so not feeling the need of English.

Never did I know, until I met that brother, how much could be said in a hand-shake. We shook hands over and over again; his said "You are welcome," mine—"I'm glad to come." I told him of a long absent brother with a hand-shake, and after forty hours exhaustion from not talking the only way I could relieve the tension was to shake him by the hand!

❦ *Alexander Selkirk (1676-1723) was a sailor who spent four years and four months as a castaway on an uninhabited island off the coast of Chile. He was rescued in 1709 and an account of his ordeal was printed in 1712. In 1719 Daniel Defoe published* **Robinson Crusoe**, *and Selkirk is supposed to be the prototype for the book.* **Robinson Crusoe** *is considered the first novel in English.*

233

Do we sense a note of triumph in this small episode?

Before leaving F. I had one inning at the train station which afforded me much gratification; a pompous looking official stepped toward me, and began a long harangue. I shrugged my shoulders to signify I did not understand, all to no purpose; when he paused for breath, I began with a rapidity and vigor of speech which a long silence can give, and talked my native tongue as never before. I chose my longest words without regard to meaning; I spoke quietly, even steadily, but so effectually that the man first stared, then backed up, and finally fled, as from a dangerous lunatic!

Dresden — Theaterplatz

Kgl. Opernhaus

Fernheizwerk

234

DRESDEN

THE JOURNEY FROM BAYREUTH TO DRESDEN seemed so much longer than we thought it ought that several times we gathered our belongings and adjusted our veils preparatory to alighting, and were only prevented from doing so by timely enquiry.

The city's second pride and glory, the famous opera house, we saw on our first night there, when we listened to Perron's fine impersonation of the principal character in Rubenstein's seldom given, but intensely striking opera *The Demon*. It is difficult to understand why this work is so rarely heard; the music is most expressive, the Demon's love song haunting one for days, while the situations are powerful and the libretto unusually strong.

We can easily understand Americans delighting in an extended stay in Dresden—especially music lovers, who can hear fine singers in the best operas for the trifling sum of twenty-five cents; and how artists must revel in the great picture gallery!

Dresden
Kgl. Residenz-Schloss   Georgentor

Dresden — Brühl'sche Terrasse

Dresden — Nymphenbad im Kgl. Zwinger

Dresden — Postplatz

Dresden.   Schlossübergang nach der kath. Hofkirche.

I spend the Sunday here in
No meet me in   Dresden.
Wernigerode

No stranger goes to Dresden but is tempted to spend hours in "Der grosser Garten," wandering down the shady paths feeling as if in far off woods, miles from any dwelling.

One Sunday afternoon we went to see a German holiday, a "Blumen Fest." Thousands of men and women were there, dressed in their best, taking their pleasure as they do their beer, deliberately and sedately. Bicycles decorated with flowers, their riders costumed in hues to match, were in competition for the race. On the lake boats were adorned with flowers, and bowers of roses erected, under which sat plump German Mädchen. Lotteries faced one at every few steps, and although on principle one objects, everything was done quietly and in order. Even the children played noiselessly, without the clamor which the average American child considers necessary to a good time.

BERLIN

A TRYING FEATURE OF SIGHTSEEING is the constant change of abode involved. One just begins to feel at home, to be familiar with the streets and houses, to make agreeable acquaintances, when that relentless inexorable tyrant—Time, tells us we must move.

"No parks will seem so green, no people so friendly, no place as desirable as Dresden," I said sadly the morning we left for Berlin, and E mournfully agreed.

In the afternoon we both blushed for our fickleness, in that we found the great capital still more fascinating!

In every place we have been able to find our way with but little difficulty, directions being given us most kindly and explicitly invariably concluding with "you can't possibly miss it." Before we knew ourselves as intimately as we now do, this gave us great encouragement, but in an early stage of our career in Deutschland, we decided that Germans did not realize the talent we possesses for going wrong, for we quite frequently managed to "miss it" at the outset.

Consequently, the good natured Frau was not to blame, because after careful explanations as to the electrics we were to take for Charlottenburg, we chased one for a half mile only to be told that our way lay in the opposite direction. Imagine riding miles on street cars, through seemingly endless parks, seeing on each side inviting footpaths winding in and out among the trees.

We did our duty by the schloss, but later, whispered to each other—so faintly that the walls were none the wiser—"what a bore to look at endless old paintings of Margraves and Margravines, whose names if ever known, are now forgotten."

It was a relief to leave the Castle and walk down the board pathway, lined with trees and marble busts, to the mausoleum, the entrance to which is most impressive. Here lies the old Kaiser Wilhelm and Empress Augusta, and beside them the Emperor's Father and Mother, the latter the famous Queen Louise, the loveliest of all German women.

The Angel of the tomb—a heroic figure in white marble—stands with drawn sword a few feet from the door, while through deep azure glass a dim religious light is shed which causes idle talk to cease, and makes one's foot steps lightly fall about that hallowed spot.

Berlin — National-Gallerie und Friedrichs-Brücke

Berlin — Palais Kaiser Wilhelm I. — Unter den Linden. — Universität

Comparing Notes

AFTER OUR VISIT TO POTSDAM we gathered around the festive board at evening tea and compared notes. We found that the other guests had previously visited Sans Souci— where the great Frederic and Voltaire had lived for a time on such familiar terms—and had, as well as we, seen the fountains send up streams of water 140 feet into the air.

Gruss aus Sanssouci-Potsdam

Neues Palais

Potsdam Ruinenberg. Reservoir für die Fontaine von Sanssouci (Inhalt 5 000 000 Liter)

242

Göttingen.   Partie Reinhausen-Bremke.

Respite in Gottingen

THE ADVANTAGES OF GREAT CITIES are always appreciated, but the quietness and restfulness of Gottingen is most thoroughly enjoyed when one has been for months in crowded places.

Gottingen like other university towns depends upon its 1600 students, more or less, for all its life. When in summer they are gone, the stillness can be felt. The many plain stone buildings attracted us, where during winter months the learned Herr professors lecture.

We climbed one of the surrounding hills for views of tiny villages, and far off distant haze of blue Hartz Mountains, while nearer wooded road, and land with ripened crops, gave different aspect.

The path on which we walked was lined with purple plum trees; "these are annually auctioned to the poor" explained our hostess, "who for a merely nominal sum tend them, and later sell the fruit." "Is it never stolen?" I enquired, as visions of too early gathered pears, and ground strewn thick with green grapes came before me. "Never, Germans are invariably honest," was the unqualified assertion.

The quiet beauty of German landscape is well seen on the way from Gottingen to Frankfort. One passes village after village, whose red-roofed houses form a pleasing contrast to the green of many trees—large flocks of geese driven by the barefooted goose-girl was a feature which attracted me.

I saw with mine own eyes five women at work sawing and splitting a large pile of wood. Again, they or their sisters bore the heat and burden of the day working in the fields beside the men, and later bending under heavy loads.

Göttingen   Gauss-Weber-Denkmal.

It is a terrible temptation "to linger at each enticing town."

When we reached Bedra we succumbed, and branched off to have a peep at Eisenach, where we climbed, by carriage, the picturesque Wartburg, the home of holy St. Elizabeth. While descending we passed the cave where daily she fed the hungry poor, and through one opening in the trees we had a glimpse of distant Venusberg. Each new sight recalled and made more impressive Wagner's immortal *Tannhäuser*.

We passed before Bach's birthplace, and in the doorway stood the present tenant, who made us welcome. Although the house is not always shown to strangers he allowed us to stand in the very room where the Father of Instrumental Music voiced his first prelude to a life of earnest work and purpose.

☾ *Mrs Kotzschmar writes here about Wartburg Castle, situated on a precipitous hill overlooking the town of Eisenach in Thuringia. The castle was founded in 1067 by the landgrave Ludwig the Springer.*

Ludwig IV, heir to Wartburg, married Elizabeth of Hungary (1207-1231). While married and then as a widow, she continually gave away her wealth to the poor, distributing food and even building hospitals. She was canonized soon after her death, and is the patron saint of hospitals, nurses, bakers, brides, dying children and widows. She is a symbol of Christian charity.

*The mythological mountain Venusberg is another name for the actual mountain called Hörselberg. When Mrs. Kotzschmar glimpsed Hörselberg through the trees, she was reminded of Wagner's opera **Tannhäuser.***

FRANZ VON LISZT

BIRTHPLACE

REWARD CARD

Wiemar the Beautiful

H<small>ERE CAN BE FOUND</small> another "Belvedere" whose gently sloping driveway with old trees, whose interlacing branches meet o'erhead, and form a canopy to shield from sun and rain, brought us to see with eager eyes the spot where art and nature vied to make an ideal theatre. There Goethe, Schiller, with other mighty poets enacted years ago their famous plays.

We walked through the length and the breadth of Weimar with delight; her museum, which in spite of the prefix of Goethe, truth compels us to state we found but a 'museum' still. It was so bare and comfortless, it had so little atmosphere of home we could not realize that there, once met and talked together day after day, a prince of poets and a prince of men.

The place of places in all Weimar that I longed to see was Liszt's home. His faithful housekeeper for thirty years met me at the door and though I could not utter words, there was a nameless speech of sympathy between us, which made us not, as strangers. She showed me where her master lived his daily life, ate, drank and slept. I held the manuscript he wrote, and laid my hand with reverence on that instrument that never more will answer to his wondrous touch.

❦ *"Belvedere" is the Italian word for beautiful view; the term was applied to buildings such as castles, and also to small pavilions or towers on top of buildings or hills which commanded a panoramic view.*

In Frankfurt

I HAVE THE INCLINATION BUT NOT SPACE to tell of Frankfurt's marble Ariadne so exquisite in conception, so masterful in execution, or of the pleasures of her Palm garden where music blends with nature in such perfect harmony.

The romance of old Heidelberg, its ruined castle, of these I cannot speak, nor yet of lofty Königstuhl, where far below I saw the Neckar winding in and out through meadows green.

In the distance a silvery thread-like stream I knew was Father Rhine, and by its shores was Mannheim, and here I was to find what I had longed for—my German Schwester—the joy, the happiness of that meeting I have not power to tell, and so as I began this letter so end I.

❅ *This is the end of Letter 22, the beginning of which was Mrs. Kotzschmar's visit to her husband's birthplace, Finsterwalde. In Mannheim she met her husband's younger sister (schwester), Christine Auguste, who was born in Finsterwalde on July 28, 1831.*

Frankfurt a. M.   Ariadne Rückansicht

250

GROSSHERZOGIN LUISE U. GROSSHERZOG FRIEDRICH VON BADEN

"A Glimpse of the German Kaiser"

"Remain in Mannheim over Monday, and you shall see a Rheinfest, with something that can be seen nowhere else in all the world." This was said in excellent English by one of our German relatives the day we had planned to leave them; our inclination prompted us to "remain" and the mysterious "something" finally decided us.

The reason for the celebration was the visit of the Grand Duke of Baden, and on such occasions a short, triumphal trip upon the Rhine is invariably made. Invitations by card were issued days before.

We, having choice of two steamers, started early to make selection of the best. We found between twenty and thirty large steam ships anchored in line upon the river, and one mass of fluttering flags of every combination of colors; wreaths of green mingled with flowers were festooned completely around the vessels; bands of music played *The Watch on the Rhine,* and similar exhilarating airs.

Rhine water flowed beneath us, and Rhine wine, scarcely stronger, flowed freely on board ship. The elite of Mannheim chatted with the many officers while nibbling German cakes and all waited patiently for the booming of the 200 guns which were to announce the arrival of the Duke.

"There he is!" we all cried as a terrific crash came, and immediately the largest ship moved along the water, and we saw an elderly man with many medals bowing acknowledgement of the deafening cheers from the multitude that lined the shores.

The sight of sights however, came when we were opposite the largest manufactory of aniline dyes in the world. Pipes containing different colored dyes were laid along the bed of the river, and as the Duke's ship started the waters of the Rhine were forced through them and into the air nearly one hundred feet, showing the most exquisite coloring, pale pink deepening to darkest shade of crimson then fading, to be replaced by faintest tints of yellow, deepening gradually to sulphur, then giving way to blue-purple-green in every known shade. The water for a long distance was tinged with the different hues and it all made a charming and most unusual spectacle.

251

"Unique and Interesting Celebrations at Mannheim"

THERE ARE THOSE WHO DECLARE THAT MANNHEIM is most uninteresting with its regular straight lines of streets, its many "Fabriken" as the manufactories are termed; but, like other things, that depends upon one's point of view. To us it was the most homelike spot in Europe-- the shops attractive, the opera fine, its people as our own people.

Its public park, not only beautiful to look upon, but practically beneficial to the children has a large portion reserved as a play ground. There every sort of sport is furnished for tiny tots as well as boys and girls of twelve. A man in charge assists in stretching nets for tennis, or in placing croquet wickets, and also sees all rights protected. At four o'clock, fresh milk and bread is served for the children at a trifling cost. While sitting at tables beneath the trees, the mothers talk, sew and drink chocolate.

Feeling we were leaving a place grown very dear, reluctantly we said "auf wiedersehen" to Mannheim and began our Rhine trip.

It was early in the morning when we left Mannheim, and although the sun was shining it was a chilly wintry smile accompanied by a blustering breeze. When on board the *Lohengrin* we tried to warm ourselves with our enthusiasm, but found it utterly lacking the caloric stored in coal, so crept up close beside the smoke stack, and thus shielded, we began to watch the changing panorama with ever increasing pleasure.

The charm of clustering villages, the grandeur of high precipices, the romance and the poetry of the Rhine, made us forget ourselves in dreaming meditation from which we were awakened by the hissing of a locomotive. As the train rushed by, along the very shore of the river, we said, "It never can be as it was, increasing traffic dulls the halo that surrounds these ideal places;" and we did not wonder that the Lorelei left her rocky height when it was desecrated by being blasted for a tunnel.

BONN   Rheinbrücke

254

BONN AND BEETHOVEN

AT **BONN WE BROKE OUR JOURNEY** for two reasons, the first prosaic as it was to try and thaw, if possible, our frozen frames.

It is never wise to judge the customs of a country too hastily. Time—and weather—works wonders. We feel that the only opportunity for offering reparation to the feather-comforters of Germany lies through the columns of the *Daily Press*; therefore apologetically we recall the gibes, the scoffs and sneers with which before our Rhine voyage we cast those feather beds away.

Can we forget that night in Bonn when thankfully we used them? They brought delicious warmth and lightness, like feathery coals of fire, upon two chilled and thoroughly repentant beings.

BONN   Beethovens Geburtshaus (Gartenseite)

256

Bonn.

Ludwig van Beethoven's Geburtszimmer.

BONN MEANS FOR US—BEETHOVEN—and the one pilgrimage we had looked forward to making was to visit that great musician's birthplace.

We stood inside a bare chamber, with low ceiling, containing only the marble bust of Music's genius—Beethoven. Pictures without number lined the walls of another room presenting as many different faces as those of Avon's bard.

Personal belongings were exhibited, and most pathetic were the brazen ear-trumpets of varying designs and sizes; these told us, if dumbly, not less vividly and touchingly of the great Master's sore affliction.

TALL TALES IN COLOGNE

THE BOAT-RIDE TO COLOGNE may be all that is most desirable in mid-summer, but in September, under foggy skies and with an almost zero temperature, we missed greatly the charm of scenery that lies between Mannheim and Bonn, and gladly left the steamer to gain a view of Germany's most wonderful cathedral.

The dizzy heights to which those spires rise, the carvings delicate as tracery—the infinite variety of figures—these we looked at over and over again, and as we looked the wonder of it all came to us more and more.

We grieve to say our faith was not even as a grain of mustard seed when told that the shrine contained the skulls of the three Magi. It stood the test, however, when assured that where we walked about in St. Ursula's Church, eleven thousand virgins lost their lives in barbarous times, and all their bones were used to fresco walls and ceilings. But when the priest declared the broken vessel which we saw was the identical one used at the marriage feast in Cana of Gailee, then our faith vanished as chaff blown before the wind.

THROUGH BRUSSELS AND ON TO "A BRIEF GLANCE AT HOLLAND"

260

THE FIRST INTIMATION WE RECEIVED that summer and our days were waning was on the Rhine; the next came while we were covering the distance from Cologne to Brussels.

"You will certainly arrive by seven o'clock" the wily ticket seller told us, ignoring the hour's difference in time, which when we reached the Belgian frontier compelled us to put back our hour hand just 60 minutes. Darkness was all about us as we alighted from the train, and we felt a pang assail our hearts, for well we knew that shortened daylight meant an ended holiday.

We found Brussels even more wide awake and bustling than is its usual habit, owing to the exposition to which we gave our forenoon. The grounds were pleasing, and when lighted by electric lights the many colored globes made the effect most brilliant. The exhibition seemed rather ordinary, after the White City's dazzling array.

We found greater satisfaction and enjoyment in driving about the broad tree-lined avenues of this "little Paris" and looking at the Hotel de Ville and stupendous Palais du Justice, which we could well believe the largest building in the world.

262

"WE MUST HURRY ON TO HOLLAND," remarked W with decision, the day following our excursion to Waterloo, "or we shall never have time to see as many windmills as we wish."

In consequence of this strong desire for Dutch landmarks, our stay in Antwerp was only long enough to let us see the crowning work of Rubens—his *Descent from the Cross*, and when we looked on that we felt that we had never before seen the true Rubens. The gross high-colored women all were gone and only grief and the end of the Great Sacrifice were shown with almost superhuman power.

ANVERS. — La Descente de Croix, par P. P. Rubens à la Cathédrale
ANTWERPEN. — De Kruisafdoening, door P. P. Rubens in de
Hoofdkerk.

263

264

Volendam

THE CLEANLINESS AND THE BEAUTY OF THE HAGUE appealed to us as it does to everyone.

The clumsy wooden shoes, which even babies wear, made our feet ache from sympathy, while the caps and headgear of the women with their gold and silver ornaments baffle description. The effect was very ludicrous when some old dames wearing spreading lace-like wings on each side of their heads, and a sort of plaited curtain hanging down their backs, surmounted the whole with somewhat modern bonnets.

Delft Markt op Marktdag

WE FOUND EVERYTHING as quaint and picturesque as we had hoped, but most expensive. With childlike confidence we went to Delft expecting, for a song, to buy some souvenirs; not so, they cost as much as in America.

But if we could not secure porcelain, we gained many a peaceful landscape of flat green pastures, where innumerable Dutch cattle grazed, and countless windmills waved their long arms, seemingly in farewell.

SCHEVENINGEN
Gezicht op Strand en Kurhaus

268

"BATHING AT SCHEVENINGEN"

O N ONE OF THE LOVELIEST OF EARLY SEPTEMBER DAYS we visited Scheveningen.

The beach was lined with wheeled bath houses; when hired, the temporary tenant enters, then the horse is harnessed and drags all into the water; when arrayed, the bather walks down three of four steps into the briny deep, without the least exposure to the public gaze. This seemed to us a much more agreeable fashion for surf bathing than we have at home.

Children were building sand forts. Young people were sauntering on the beach, while older ones were sitting in what looked like wicker bath tubs standing on end. They were in reality chairs, and the large hood made most comfortable protection from the sun and wind. We queried why some enterprising New Englander had not introduced them at Old Orchard.

☾ *Old Orchard is a beach and resort area just south of Portland, Maine. The Kotzschmar family used to spend some time each summer in a cottage nearby.*

"Pleasure and Ease of Foreign Travel"

WE HAVE A LURKING CONSCIOUSNESS, as we near the completion of our tour, that we have enjoyed each different country in turn, with much the same zest that one of Mrs. Barbauld's* old-time heroines reveled in the seasons.

That impressionable young person walked forth with her mother when Earth renews its youth, and budding leaf and running brook make her declare she loves the springtime best; but soon the song of birds and blossoming of flowers transport her with delight, and she is positive no season equals summer. Then come the nuts and ripened fruits of fall and she is sure these months exceed them all; till skating, sleighing and the joys of Christmas make it plain that winter reigns triumphant in her heart.

And so it is with us, we find it difficult to choose, for each in turn seems best; and yet perhaps for all in all, the most enjoyable portion of our European trip has been the time we spent in Germany, when every day brought fresh delights, and each new place seemed more alluring than the last.

The great amount of pleasure we have gained from our first peep abroad makes us eager to have our fellow-sisters enjoy a similar experience. We know there must be many women who long for Europe, as Moses did for Canaan, and fear to die without the sight; not always on account of slender purses but often from lack of courage in going alone and unprotected.

To some extent we shared these fears at first, but they soon vanished. English is so universally spoken, and more than all traveling is made easy by means of the 'International Pensions' distributed throughout the principal resorts of Europe, where for a reasonable sum comfortable accommodations can be secured for one night or longer.

*Mrs. Barbauld (1743-1825) was Anna Letitia Barbauld, a prolific English author and poet. She ran a boarding school in London with her husband and was well-known in literary circles. A two volume collected edition of her works, with a memoir, was published by her niece, Lucy Aikin, in 1825.

Rotterdam   Haven.

272

East, West, Home's Best:
"Farewell Words"

THE DAYS HAVE PASSED INTO WEEKS and weeks have lengthened into months, and now our journeyings all are ended and we are waiting in the busy seaport Rotterdam for the good ship that is to bear us home.

We've traveled many miles, seen many lands, but none more beautiful than ours. The shining Bay of Naples could not dim the beauty of fair Casco Bay; and all the wonder, all the glory we have looked upon has made us realize more keenly how wonderful, how glorious, though in a different way, is our own native land. How often since we left her shores have we rejoiced to feel we were "Americans" and owed a glad and proud allegiance to the Stars and Stripes.

☾ *Portland, Maine is situated on Casco Bay, a picturesque inlet with historic forts, scenic lighthouses and a busy waterfront.*

ROTTERDAM, DELFTSCHE VAART

Looking up Middle St., showing Fidelity Building, Portland, Me.

274

countless windmills waved their long arms, seemingly in farewell.

On one of the loveliest of early September days, we visited Scheveningen. The beach was lined with wheeled bath houses; when hired, the temporary tenant enters, then the horse is harnessed and drags all into the water; when arrayed, the bather walks down three or four steps, into the briny deep, without the least exposure to the public gaze. This seemed to us a much more agreeable fashion for surf bathing than we have at home. Children were building sand forts while older ones were sitting in what looked like wicker bath tubs standing on end, they were in reality chairs, and the large hood made most comfortable protection from the sun and wind. We queried why some enterprising New Englander had not introduced them at Old Orchard.

The great amount of pleasure we have gained from our first peep abroad, makes us eager to have our fellow-sisters enjoy a similar experience. We know there must be many women who long for Europe, as Moses did for Canaan, and fear to die without the sight; not always on account of slender purses but often from lack of courage in going alone and unprotected. To some extent we shared these fears at first, but they soon vanished. English is so universally spoken, and more than all travelling is made easy by means of the 'International Pensions' distributed throughout the principal resorts of Europe, where for a reasonable sum comfortable accommodations can be secured for one night or longer.

The days have passed into weeks, and weeks have lengthened into months, and now our journeyings are at an end and we are waiting in busy seaport Rotterdam, for the good ship that is to bear us home. We've travelled many miles, seen many lands but none more beautiful than ours. The shining Bay of Naples could not dim the beauty of fair Casco; and all the wonder, all the glory we have looked upon, but made us realize more keenly how wonderful, how glorious, though in a different way, is our own native land. How often since we left her shores have we rejoiced to feel we were 'Americans' and owed a glad and proud allegiance to the Stars and Stripes; and yet longing as we are for home and friends we could but sadly think that all the bright anticipations of a lifetime with their glad fulfillment now were ended, and as we sat in somewhat mournful mood, we felt an unseen presence and a voice murmured in our ear: "My sisters dear because their pleasant task was finished, but I have come to take their place, I am a stranger now, but hold me fast and I will be as a familiar friend, and I will never go. I'll bring again before you at your will, each cherished place; the cities large with all their treasures manifold, the snow-clad heights, the rivers and the valleys that you loved. Dimly at first they may appear, but clearer they will grow the nearer that you draw me. Still more, I have a subtle power which realization lacked, for every hour of pain and weariness or disappointment I will efface, and only peace and loveliness I'll leave." Turning, we saw a shadowy form, whose profile delicate was veiled in softest mist, and downdropt eyes seemed gazing backwards. Then with great joy we rose 'mid tears and smiles, clasping forevermore close to our hearts—Remembrance.

MRS. HERMANN KOTZSCHMAR.

In Memoriam.

The Citizens' Relief has passed these resolutions:

Since our last meeting we have been called to part with one of our most interested and devoted members, David G. Drinkwater, one of the first to join the society, and one who was always ready to promote every movement in its be-

Yet longing as we have for home and friends, we could but sadly think that all the bright anticipations of a lifetime with their glad fulfillment now were ended, and as we sat in somewhat mournful mood, we felt an unseen presence and a voice murmured in our ear—

> My sisters fled because their pleasant task was finished, but I have
> come to take their place. I am a stranger now, but hold me fast and I
> will be as a familiar friend, and I will never go. I'll bring again before
> you, at your will, each cherished place; the cities large with all their
> treasures manifold, the snow-clad heights, the rivers and the valleys
> that you loved. Dimly at first they may appear, but clearer they will
> grow the nearer that you draw me. Still more, I have a subtle power
> which realization lacked, for every hour of pain and weariness or
> disappointment I will efface, and only peace and loveliness I'll leave.

Turning, we saw a shadowy form, whose profile delicate was veiled in softest mist, and downdropt eyes seemed gazing backwards. Then, with great joy we rose, 'mid tears and smiles, clasping forevermore close to our hearts—*Remembrance*.

—Mrs. Hermann Kotzschmar
Rotterdam, 1897

Longfellow Monument, Portland, Me.

276

Lives of great men all remind us
We can make our lives sublime,
And, departing, leave behing us
Footprints in the sands of time;

Footprints, that perhaps another,
Sailing o'er life's solemn main,
A forlorn and shipwrecked brother,
Seeing, shall take heart again.

Longfellow.

❨

THIS BOOK HAS BEEN COMPOSED USING THE
TYPEFACE ADOBE GARAMOND, A MODERN DAY
INTERPRETATION OF THE ROMAN TYPES OF
CLAUDE GARAMOND AND THE ITALIC TYPES OF
ROBERT GRANJON. TYPE DESIGNER ROBERT
SLIMBACH DEVELOPED ADOBE GARAMOND IN
1989, SUCCESSFULLY CAPTURING THE BEAUTY AND
BALANCE OF THE ORIGINAL GARAMOND.

WALCH PUBLISHING OF PORTLAND PRINTED THIS
LIMITED EDITION BOOK ON 70 POUND CREAM
SPRINGHILL PAPER.

Janice Parkinson-Tucker taught public school music at all levels for thirty years. A professional musician, she has also served as an organist and church musician for more than forty years.

In 1989 she created and built a successful home business called Mrs. Bones' Decorative Dog Collars. The unique, lined collars were hand-sewn, using beautiful decorative trims imported from Europe.

In 2001 she sold her thriving business and "retired," taking on the post of Archivist for the Friends of the Kotzschmar Organ in Portland, Maine. This book is a result of her interest in music, and her passion for well-documented local history.

Janice is active in Maine as a representative for New England Airedale Rescue; she and her husband James have had Airedales for twenty years. They also share their home with 3 fourteen-year-old cats.